I'm honored to share with you some of my favorite can are experiencing some of the negative effects from candida what you're going through. I dealt with the mental fog, achy nach bloating, weight gain, and overwhelming sense of fat have experienced. This constant struggle and discomfort sparked a deep desire within me to help my body heal itself from the inside out, starting with my diet.

An integral part of my candida journey led me to Ann Boroch, author of ***Healing Multiple Sclerosis (M.S.)***. Ann healed herself from M.S. and continued helping people with Candida, M.S., Lupus, and other health issues for more than 20 years. When I began working closely with her, I came to deeply admire and trust in Ann's methods and meal plans. I witnessed profound changes in my own body and also saw these same miraculous improvements in the lives of others. Through working as a personal chef for Ann herself, I developed all of the recipes for her book, ***The Candida Cure Cookbook.***

And now I'm here to offer my recipes to you! I've provided a ton of my favorite mouthwatering breakfasts, entrées, side dishes, soups, salads, dressings and dips, as well as desserts and snacks to prepare and enjoy at your leisure. I hope that they prove to be both delicious and therapeutic. I've also included a few pages that list my suggestions for which foods to eat and which foods to avoid when sticking to an anti-candida diet. Now I know that there are lots of opinions out there about the best way to combat candida. The recipes and suggestions I provide are based on my own personal experience and the experience I've had coaching and cooking for my clients towards wellness. I always recommend listening to the advice of your doctor or medical professional.

*The recipes included are all dairy-free except for the occasional use of Unsalted, Grass-Fed Butter. Grass-fed butter is an excellent source of vitamin A. It also helps reduce inflammation in the body and helps with heart health and brain function. Some people who are mildly lactose-intolerant do fine with butter because it only contains trace amounts of lactose, but if you're really bothered by lactose, then it's a good idea to avoid butter. Instead you can opt for clarified butter (ghee) because it contains even less lactose than butter or no lactose at all.

Happy Eating!

Alison Charbonneau, Natural Tasty Chef

Natural Tasty Recipes
www.naturaltastychef.com

Sides/Snacks

"A healthy outside starts from the inside"

- *Robert Urich*

Crispy Cauliflower

Crispy Cauliflower is the perfect dish for when you're craving something fried but don't want to blow your diet.

Makes 2 – 4 servings

Ingredients:

Coconut oil
1 small head (or 1/2 large head) cauliflower

Wet ingredients:

2 eggs
1 Tablespoon unsweetened coconut or almond milk
Pinch sea salt

Dry ingredients:

1 cup coconut flour
1 cup tapioca flour
3/4 teaspoon baking powder
1/2 teaspoon smoked paprika
1/2 teaspoon garlic powder
1/2 teaspoon sea salt
Pinch black pepper

Directions:

Preheat oven to 350 degrees F. and line a baking sheet with parchment paper. Set aside.

In a medium size bowl whisk together all the dry ingredients. In a separate smaller bowl, whisk together the wet ingredients.

Heat a large skillet over medium-high heat with enough coconut oil to coat the bottom and about 1/4 inch up along the sides.

Using one hand, dredge each cauliflower floret in the egg mixture and with your other hand coat in the dry mixture. Place the cauliflower in the hot oil and allow to get crispy and golden. Turn after about 2 minutes on each side. Then, carefully remove and place on the baking sheet. Continue until all the cauliflower has been cooked. You might have to cook them in batches depending on the size of your skillet and the amount of cauliflower florets you have.

Place the baking sheet in the oven and bake for 15 – 20 minutes, or until florets are golden brown and pierceable with a fork.

I like to serve with my Spicy Mayo Dipping Sauce.

Baked Sweet Potato Fries

*Say hello to your new "fries." These **baked** fries are tender, sweet and loaded with vitamins and minerals.*

Makes 2 servings

Ingredients:
3 Tablespoons grape seed or olive oil, divided
1 large (or 2 small) organic purple, white, or orange sweet potato
1/2 teaspoon sea salt
1/8 teaspoon black pepper

Directions:
Preheat oven to 400 degrees F. and line a baking sheet with foil. Pour 1 Tablespoon grape seed or olive oil on foiled baking sheet and spread evenly, using your hands.

If organic, leave the skin of the sweet potato on. If not, peel potato first. Cut into thinly sliced fry shapes, keeping them roughly the same size for even cooking. Place in a large mixing bowl. Add remaining 2 Tablespoons grape seed or olive oil, sea salt, and black pepper. Using your hands, rub the ingredients into all of the potato slices. Place them onto baking sheet, trying not to overlap.

Bake fries for about 15 - 20 minutes. Remove from the oven and flip the fries using a spatula. Return to oven and continue baking for about 5 - 10 minutes more or until they are cooked to your liking. Once you have removed the fries from the oven, give them a few minutes to cool and to become crispier.

I like serving with Homemade Ketchup.

*

Sweet and Salty Kabocha Squash Slices

Kabocha squash, sometimes referred to as Japanese pumpkin, is the sweetest of all the squashes! It gets very soft when cooked and makes the most delicious snack or soup. The key to picking the perfect kabocha squash is the shape of the squash and the color of its markings. You want it to be horizontally oval in shape and to have a round yellow/orange marking on it.

Makes 4 servings

Ingredients:
Olive or coconut oil spray
1 medium size kabocha squash
1/4 cup olive or grape seed oil
1 Tablespoon xylitol
1 teaspoon cinnamon
1/2 teaspoon sea salt

Directions:
Preheat oven to 400 degrees F. Generously spray a baking sheet with coconut or olive oil spray. Cut washed squash in half lengthwise, remove the seeds, and slice each half into 1/8 - 1/4-inch wedges. Place in a medium-size mixing bowl.

In a small bowl or measuring cup, mix together the oil, xylitol, cinnamon and sea salt. Pour over the squash, coating the pieces well, using your hands.

*

Place the squash on the prepared baking sheet and bake for 10 minutes. Remove from the oven and flip the slices over with a spatula. Continue baking for another 5 minutes or until desired crispness is reached.

Mashed Yams or Sweet Potato

Although yams and sweet potatoes are often used interchangeably, they are actually two different vegetables. Yams are orange in color and get much softer and sweeter when cooked. They are shown in the picture below, but both work well for this recipe.

Makes 2 servings

Ingredients:
2 cups chopped yam or sweet potato, (If organic, keep skin on)
4 - 6 garlic cloves
1 – 1/2 cups unsweetened coconut milk, more if necessary
1/4 teaspoon sea salt
2 Tablespoons unsalted, grass-fed butter
Pinch black pepper

Directions:
Place the chopped sweet potato and whole garlic cloves in a medium sized saucepan with coconut milk and sea salt. Add more coconut milk if necessary, to just about cover the sweet potatoes. Bring the liquid to a boil, then cover and reduce heat to medium. Simmer for about 10 – 12 minutes, or until the sweet potato can be easily pierced with a fork. Cooking time will vary depending on the size cut of your sweet potato.

Once the sweet potato is tender, remove from heat. If there is still a lot of liquid in your pot, carefully remove the sweet potato using a slotted spoon, avoiding the cooking liquid, and place potatoes and garlic in a medium size mixing bowl. Add the butter and using a potato masher, mash everything together, being sure to break up the garlic cloves. Add black pepper and taste for seasoning.

The BEST Cauliflower & Sweet Potato Mash

I know naming something the BEST is pretty bold, but so are these Cauliflower and Sweet Potato Mashies! They're rich, creamy and healthy for you too. They're a side dish you can feel good about feeding to yourself and your family.

Makes 4 servings

Ingredients:
2 cups white sweet potato*, washed and cubed
3 cups cauliflower, chopped
6 cloves garlic
1 (13.5-ounce) can coconut milk
1/4 teaspoon sea salt, more if desired
Filtered water
4 Tablespoons grass-fed butter
Pinch black pepper
2 green onions, minced

Directions:
In a medium sized saucepan add the sweet potato, cauliflower, garlic, coconut milk, and sea salt. Add filtered water to just cover the top of the veggies. Bring to a boil, cover with a fitted lid, and reduce heat to medium-low. Simmer for 10 – 15 minutes, or until the sweet potato is pierceable with a fork. Remove from heat.

If there is excess liquid, use a slotted spoon to remove the potatoes, cauliflower, and garlic cloves from the saucepan and place in a large mixing bowl. Add the butter and black pepper. Using a potato masher, mash until creamy and everything is fully incorporated. Option to use a hand mixer at this point.

Mix in the green onions and taste for seasoning. Add more salt if necessary.

If sweet potato is organic, no need to peel.

Baked Veggies

Baked veggies make a great side for any dish. My favorite way to serve them is beside Quinoa Tabbouleh with Guacamole or Zesty Ranch.

Makes 2 – 4 servings

Ingredients:
3 Tablespoons olive oil, divided
2 green zucchinis
1 yellow zucchini
2 medium size carrots
1 cup chopped broccoli
1 yellow onion, large chop
6 whole garlic cloves
1/4 teaspoon sea salt
1/8 teaspoon black pepper
Zest and juice of 1 lemon

Directions:
Preheat oven to 300 degrees F. Line a baking sheet with foil or parchment paper and drizzle with 1 Tablespoon of olive oil.

Chop green and yellow zucchini into large chunks, with skin on, if organic. The carrots will be the firmest of the vegetables and will take the longest to cook, therefore cut the carrots into smaller slices or wheels.

Place chopped green and yellow zucchini into a large mixing bowl along with the chopped carrots, chopped broccoli, chopped onion, and whole garlic cloves. Drizzle with the remaining 2 Tablespoons of olive oil, sea salt, pepper and lemon zest and stir with a wooden spoon to evenly coat the vegetables. Place veggies on the lined baking sheet and bake for 15 minutes. Remove from the oven, give the veggies a quick stir and bake for another 10 minutes, or until veggies are tender and pierceable with a fork.

Remove from oven and drizzle with lemon juice. Serve warm.

Deviled Eggs

My mother always made deviled eggs for the 4th of July. And although they might seem like cookout food, they actually make a great snack all year round.

Makes 12 halves

Ingredients:
6 hard boiled eggs
2 – 3 Tablespoons ***Homemade Mayonnaise (see recipe)***
1/4 teaspoon smoked paprika, more for garnish
Generous pinch sea salt
Pinch black pepper

Directions:
Using a slightly wet knife cut each egg in half. Carefully remove the yolk of each egg and add to a mixing bowl. Add the remaining ingredients to the same bowl and use a fork to combine. You can also use a hand mixer to get the consistency nice and smooth. Taste for seasoning.

Carefully add a scoop of filling back into the center of each egg. Garnish with a dusting of smoked paprika.

Brown Rice

The more you chew brown rice, the sweeter it gets. It might sound silly but chewing brown rice really well can help you curb sweet cravings. Here's a basic brown rice recipe that will help you achieve the perfect pot every single time.

Makes about 2 cups

Ingredients:
1 cup short grain brown rice*
2 cups filtered water
Pinch sea salt

Directions:
Rinse the rice in a fine mesh strainer under cool water. Place in small sauce pot with a fitted lid; add filtered water and a pinch of sea salt. Bring to a boil over high heat, cover with a fitted lid and reduce the heat to low. Simmer for 40 minutes. Turn off the heat and let sit for another 5 minutes before removing the lid. (This step prevents sticking). Remove lid and fluff with a fork.

Cooking time will vary depending on size of the grain; read package instructions.

Sautéed Collard Greens

Collard greens don't seem to get as much press as kale, and I'm not sure why. They are equally nutritious, and I find them softer, easier to digest and less bitter. This recipe is my favorite way to prepare collards.

Makes 2 – 3 servings

Ingredients:
8 collard green leaves, washed
1 Tablespoon olive oil
1/2 medium size yellow onion, cut into half moons
3 garlic cloves, minced
1 Tablespoon fresh ginger, peeled and minced
3 pinches sea salt
1 Tablespoon apple cider vinegar
2 Tablespoons sunflower seeds, pumpkin seeds or slivered almonds

Directions:
Remove the stems from the collared green leaves carefully using a knife. Finely chop the stems into small pieces and set aside. Stack collard green leaves and cut them into bite size pieces.

Heat a large skillet over medium heat and add the olive oil. Add the onions, garlic, ginger, and a pinch of sea salt and sauté for 3 - 4 minutes, until the onions start to break down and get soft. Next add the finely chopped collard stems, another pinch of sea salt, and sauté for a couple of minutes more. Now add the collard leaves, apple cider vinegar and a final pinch of sea salt and cover with a fitted lid. Let the steam created from the apple cider vinegar wilt the leaves slightly. This should only take about 2 - 3 minutes.

Remove lid, turn off the heat, and add the seeds or almonds. Enjoy warm.

Avocado and Cucumber Salad

Avocado and Cucumber Salad is one of my favorite snacks around. The soft and buttery avocado combined with crisp cucumber is light and refreshing yet totally satisfying. I make this for my personal chef clients almost every week.

Makes 2 servings

Ingredients:
4 Persian cucumbers, medium dice
2 ripe avocados, diced
1/3 cup red onion, minced
1/4 cup black olives, chopped
1/4 cup fresh cilantro, minced
2 Tablespoons olive oil
1 Tablespoon brown rice vinegar or apple cider vinegar
Juice of 1 lemon or lime
2 drops liquid stevia
Pinch sea salt and black pepper

Directions:
Place cucumbers, avocado, red onion, black olives and cilantro in a medium to large mixing bowl.

In a separate small bowl, whisk together the olive oil, brown rice or apple cider vinegar, lemon or lime juice, stevia, sea salt, and black pepper. Pour some of the dressing over the cucumber mixture and gently stir to combine.

Taste for seasoning; add more dressing if desired.

Asian Coleslaw

This simple, yet flavorful coleslaw recipe is ready in minutes. Whenever I'm serving tacos, this coleslaw is always on the side.

Makes 3 – 4 servings

Ingredients:

Slaw:

2 cups green cabbage, shredded
1 cup purple cabbage, shredded*
1 carrot, grated
2 Tablespoons green onions, finely chopped
1/2 teaspoon sea salt
2 Tablespoons cilantro, minced
2 Tablespoons raw sesame seeds

Dressing:

2 Tablespoons sesame oil
1 Tablespoon fresh lime juice
1 Tablespoon apple cider vinegar
4 drops liquid stevia
Pinch sea salt

Directions:

Place the cabbage, carrot and green onions into a large mixing bowl and sprinkle with 1/2 teaspoon of sea salt. Using your hands, massage the sea salt into the mixture to break it down. You will notice the cabbage start to get softer. Now add the cilantro and sesame seeds.

In a small mixing bowl, whisk together the dressing ingredients and then pour over the coleslaw. Mix everything together and enjoy.

Option to use all green cabbage.

Soups

"It is health that is the real wealth and not pieces of gold and silver."

- *Mahatma Gandhi*

Creamy Carrot, Ginger Soup

In my personal chef business, this creamy carrot ginger soup gets requested on a weekly basis. And as you'll see, I use simple ingredients that come together in perfect harmony. This totally plant-based soup is filling, satisfying, slightly sweet and SO delicious!

Makes 4 servings

Ingredients:
6 - 8 medium size carrots* (1 pound), chopped
1 yellow onion, diced
1 (1-inch) piece of ginger, peeled and diced
1 (14-ounce) can of whole fat or light coconut milk
Filtered water
1/8 teaspoon sea salt
1 teaspoon ground cinnamon

Directions:
Place carrots, onion, ginger, and coconut milk into a medium to large saucepan and add just enough filtered water to almost cover the vegetables. Add the sea salt and bring to a boil and then reduce heat to low. Cover and simmer until carrots are soft, about 15 minutes.

Transfer to a blender. Add ground cinnamon and blend until smooth and creamy. Season to taste.

No need to peel carrots if they are organic. If not, peel carrots first.

Cream of Broccoli Soup

This vegan, plant-based soup is so simple to make. It's creamy, comforting and nutrient dense. Soups are an easy way to add more vegetables into your diet on a regular basis.

Makes 4 servings

Ingredients:
4 cups chopped broccoli
1 yellow onion, diced
3 garlic cloves
1 (14-ounce) can of whole fat or light coconut milk
Filtered water
1/4 teaspoon sea salt
Pinch black pepper
2 Tablespoons sunflower seeds, for garnish

Directions:
Place broccoli, onion, garlic, and coconut milk into a medium to large saucepan and add just enough filtered water to almost cover the vegetables. Add sea salt and bring to a boil and then reduce heat to low. Cover and simmer until vegetables are soft, about 10 minutes.

Transfer to a blender. Add black pepper and blend until smooth and creamy. Season to taste.

Enjoy garnished with a sprinkle of sunflower seeds.

*

Rosemary, Cauliflower Soup

This soup is thick, creamy and packed with flavor. It's nutrient dense and ready in about 15 minutes. Perfect for cold and lazy nights.

Makes 4 servings

Ingredients:
4 cups chopped cauliflower
1 yellow onion, diced
3 garlic cloves
1 teaspoon dried or fresh rosemary, more for garnish
1 Tablespoon olive oil
1 (14-ounce) can of whole fat or light coconut milk
Filtered water
1/4 teaspoon sea salt
Pinch black pepper, for garnish
2 Tablespoons sunflower seeds, for garnish (optional)

Directions:
Place cauliflower, onion, garlic, rosemary, olive oil and coconut milk into a medium to large saucepan and add just enough filtered water to almost cover the vegetables. Add sea salt and bring to a boil and then reduce heat to low. Cover and simmer until vegetables are soft, about 15 minutes.

Transfer to a blender and blend until smooth and creamy. Season to taste.

Enjoy garnished with a pinch of black pepper, fresh rosemary, and a sprinkle of sunflower seeds.

*

Sweet Potato, Leek and Onion Soup

If you haven't noticed by now, I love pairing leeks and onions together. Adding sweet potato to this recipe really rounds it out. This recipe calls for white sweet potato, but orange yams would be equally delicious.

Makes 4 servings

Ingredients:
2 Tablespoons olive oil or grass-fed butter
3 - 4 medium leeks (about 4 cups), (green and white parts), washed and sliced*
2 medium size yellow onions, chopped
1 cup white sweet potato, diced to small pieces**
1/2 teaspoon salt
1/8 teaspoon pepper
1-quart (32-ounces) vegetable broth (no sugar added)
1 Tablespoon green onions, chopped

Directions:
In a medium to large soup pot, heat olive oil or butter over medium heat. Add leeks, onions and potato, and stir to coat the veggies with the oil. Season with salt and pepper, cover pan and let vegetables sweat over very low heat for about 5 minutes.

Next, add the vegetable broth and bring to a light boil. Cover with a fitted lid and simmer gently for about 20 minutes, or until vegetables are soft.

Remove from heat and remove the cover. Let cool for about 10 minutes before transferring to a high-powered blender. Cover and blend, starting on a low speed and gradually increasing to a high speed.

Serve and garnish with chopped green onions. Season to taste.

To clean leeks: Slice the leek in half (length-wise) and then slice in small half-moons on a slight diagonal. Place half-moon slices in a colander and rinse under water. This method cleans the dirt hidden within the many layers of leeks.
*****If potato is organic, wash and leave skin on. If not, peel skin first before chopping. If a white sweet potato is hard to find, substitute an orange sweet potato.***

Creamy Butternut Squash Soup

This soup brings me back to culinary school. It's so simple to make, yet out of this world delicious. As you eliminate refined sugars from your diet, you'll start to appreciate the natural sweetness of vegetables such as butternut squash.

Makes 4 servings

Ingredients:
1 Tablespoon coconut oil
1 medium size yellow onion, roughly chopped
1/8 teaspoon sea salt
About 2 and 1/2 cups butternut squash, peeled and cut in 1-inch chunks*
1 (14-ounce) can of whole fat or light coconut milk
1/2 teaspoon ground cinnamon, more for garnish
Filtered water

Directions:
Place a large saucepan over medium high heat and add 1 Tablespoon coconut oil. Add the onions and sea salt and sauté for 2 - 3 minutes. Then add the butternut squash, coconut milk, cinnamon, and filtered water to just cover the vegetables.

Bring the liquid to a boil. Once boiling, cover and reduce heat to medium-low. Simmer for about 10 – 15 minutes, or until the squash has softened.

Remove from heat and remove lid. Let cool for a couple of minutes and then transfer to a high-powered blender. Blend, starting on low speed and increasing to high speed. Remember that the liquid will be hot, so be careful! Blend until smooth and creamy. Taste for seasoning and if too thick, add more water and blend some more.

Enjoy garnished with a pinch of cinnamon.

If you prefer a thicker soup, add more butternut squash, totaling about 3 cups, and go easy on the filtered water. You can always add more water in the blender if the texture is too thick.

Thai Spiced Lentil Soup

Red lentils are a great source of protein and also inexpensive. When cooked, they become soft and creamy. This dish comes together in under 20 minutes. It's one of those delicious recipes that you'll want to make over and over again.

Makes 4 servings

Ingredients:
1 Tablespoon coconut oil
1 large yellow onion, diced
4 garlic cloves, minced
1 (1-inch) piece fresh ginger, peeled and minced
1 (1-inch) piece fresh turmeric, peeled and minced
1/2 teaspoon sea salt, divided
1/4 teaspoon ground cinnamon
1 teaspoon dried cumin
1/2 teaspoon black pepper
1 cup celery, small dice
1 cup carrots, small dice
1 and 1/2 cups split red lentils, washed and picked through for rocks
2 teaspoons red curry paste
1 (14-ounce can) coconut milk
4 cups filtered water
2 cups kale leaves, chopped
2 Tablespoons cilantro, minced for garnish

*

Directions:
In a large stock or soup pot, heat coconut oil over medium heat and add yellow onion, garlic, ginger, turmeric, 1/4 teaspoon of sea salt, cinnamon, cumin, and black pepper. Sauté for 3 – 4 minutes. Next add the celery and carrots and sauté for about 3 minutes more.

Now add the split red lentils, red curry paste, coconut milk, filtered water and 1/4 teaspoon sea salt and bring to a boil. Cover with a fitted lid and reduce heat to low. Simmer for about 10 – 12 minutes, or until lentils are tender.

Finally add chopped kale, give it a stir and cook for 1 minute more. Serve garnished with cilantro.

I like serving with Brown Rice.

Garlic Roasted Beef Bone Marrow Broth

Bone Broth is extremely beneficial for restoring gut health. It's thought to help heal and seal the gut lining. When your gut is healthy, your immune system is stronger, and you absorb and utilize your food more efficiently.

Makes about 6 – 10 cups

Ingredients:
2 heads garlic
1/2-pound grass-fed beef marrow bones
1 Tablespoon olive oil
2 pinches sea salt, divided
1 large carrot, rough chop
1 onion, cut into large chunks
2 ribs (sticks) celery, cut into chunks
8 cups filtered water
slow cooker

Directions:
Preheat oven to 350 degrees F. Without peeling or peeling away any cloves, cut the tops off the bunches of garlic and place them with the marrow bones on a cookie sheet (with a lip to catch fat drippings). Drizzle with olive oil and sprinkle with sea salt. Bake for 10 minutes.

In the meantime, place the chopped carrot, chopped onion, and celery in your slow cooker with another pinch of sea salt.

Once the bones are done baking, remove from the oven and place in the slow cooker along with all of the fat and juices that may have dripped off onto the cookie sheet and the garlic.

Set your slow cooker to low and let simmer from 24 – 48 hours. The longer the broth is cooked, the more flavorful it gets. Once finished simmering, strain and keep the broth and discard the bones and vegetables.

Store broth in mason jars with fitted lids in the fridge for up to one week or in the freezer for up to 2 months. If freezing, make sure to allow enough room in the jar for the broth to expand. This will prevent the jar from breaking.

I like serving with* Garlic, Rosemary Paleo Bread *spread with unsalted

Dips, Sauces & Dressings

"Symptoms are not enemies to be destroyed, but sacred messengers who encourage us to take better care of ourselves."

- *Food Matters*

Homemade Ketchup

I love this recipe because it always surprises people who are following very strict diets. They assume that ketchup is off the menu, then this shows up and it's like Christmas morning. A sweet and tangy healthy ketchup that's ready in minutes. No corn, sugar or high fructose corn syrup. Perfect for burgers and fries!

Makes about 1/2 cup

Ingredients:
1/4 cup tomato paste
1 Tablespoons filtered water, more if necessary
1 Tablespoon apple cider vinegar
4 drops liquid stevia
1/4 teaspoon sea salt
Pinch black pepper

Directions:
Combine all of the ingredients in a bowl and whisk with a fork. If texture is too thick, add more filtered water 1 Tablespoon at a time until desired texture if reached.

Store leftover ketchup in an airtight container with a fitted lid in the fridge for 7 – 10 days.

Vegan "Sour Cream"

This thick and creamy "sour cream" is a great addition to black bean bowls, chilis and soups.

Makes about 1 cup

Ingredients:

1 cup raw macadamia nuts, rinsed
Scant 1/4 cup filtered water, more if needed
2 Tablespoons fresh lemon juice
1 Tablespoon apple cider vinegar
1/4 teaspoon sea salt

Directions:

Place all of the ingredients into a blender. Starting on a low speed, blend slowly working up to a high speed. If the blender gets stuck, stop and scrape down the sides with a small spatula and then start on a low speed again. If it needs more liquid, add 1 Tablespoon of water at a time. Continue doing this until the "cream" is soft and velvety.

Store in an airtight container in the fridge for up to 1 week. Extra "sour cream" can be stored in the freezer in an airtight container for up to 1 month.

Brazil Nut "Parmesan Cheese"

Brazil nuts are large, crunchy and mild in flavor. I find them hearty and earthy and perfect for this recipe.

Makes 1 cup

Ingredients:
1 cup raw Brazil nuts (do not soak)
4 – 6 garlic cloves
1 teaspoon sea salt

Directions:
Rinse the Brazil nuts in a colander and set aside. Place the garlic in a food processor and pulse for a couple of seconds.

Add the Brazil nuts and sea salt, and pulse until the nuts crumble and get sticky.

Store in an airtight container in the refrigerator for up to 1 week or in the freezer for 2 – 3 months.

Note: If you cannot handle eating raw garlic, try blanching the garlic (put cloves in boiling water for 5 minutes). This will slightly alter the taste of the "cheese."

*

Guacamole

The trick to keeping guacamole green is to make sure air doesn't touch it! Transfer it to a container, cover it with plastic wrap, and press down on the plastic wrap to squeeze out any air pockets. Make sure any exposed surface of the guacamole is touching the plastic wrap, not air. This will keep the amount of browning to a minimum.

Makes about 1 cup

Ingredients:

1 large or 2 small ripe avocados, peeled and pitted
1/4 cup chopped cherry tomatoes (optional)
1 Tablespoon jalapeño pepper, finely chopped (optional)
1 Tablespoon red onion, finely chopped
1 garlic clove, smashed and minced
Juice of 1 lime
Pinch sea salt and black pepper
Fresh cilantro, minced

Directions:

Mash avocado with a fork and mix in remaining ingredients. Store leftover guacamole in an airtight container in the fridge 4 – 5 days.

Fresh Salsa

Once you learn how to make homemade salsa, you'll never go back to jarred again.

Makes about 2 cups

Ingredients:

2 Tablespoons red onion, rough chop
1 – 2 garlic cloves
1 cup cherry or grape tomatoes, diced
4 sprigs cilantro, rough chop
Juice of 1/2 lime
1 teaspoon olive oil
1 teaspoon brown rice vinegar
2 generous pinches sea salt
Pinch black pepper

Directions:

Place the red onion and garlic into a food processor and pulse 2 – 3 times. Scrape down the sides and add the remaining ingredients. Pulse a couple more times until desired texture is reached. Taste for seasoning.

Store in an airtight container with a fitted lid in the fridge for 5 - 7 days.

Spinach and Artichoke Dip

This Spinach and Artichoke Dip reminds me of Superbowl Sunday. It's rich and creamy and, of course, you can serve this dip any day of the week.

Makes about 3 - 4 cups

Ingredients:

Sunflower or Hemp Cream:

1/4 cup filtered water, more if needed
2 Tablespoons lemon juice (about 1 large or 2 small lemons)
2 Tablespoons apple cider vinegar
1 cup hemp seeds
2 cloves garlic
1/4 teaspoon sea salt

Dip:

1 Tablespoon olive oil
1/2 cup yellow onion, small dice
1/4 teaspoon sea salt, divided
3 cups frozen spinach
1 (14-ounce) can artichoke hearts, drained and chopped
Pinch black pepper

Directions:

Create the hemp seed cream by placing all of those ingredients into a blender, liquids first. Start blending on a low speed and slowly work up to a high speed until smooth and creamy. If it needs more liquid, add filtered water, 1 Tablespoon at a time, until the consistency is similar to a thick sauce.

Next, heat a large skillet over medium-high heat and add 1 Tablespoon of olive oil. Once hot, add the diced onions and a pinch of sea salt. Sauté for a couple minutes, or until onions start to soften. Add the frozen spinach and sauté for a couple minutes more. Next add the artichoke hearts and another pinch of sea salt and sauté for about 2 - 3 minutes more.

*

Finally stir in the sunflower or hemp seed cream and continue to sauté until the spinach is cooked and all the ingredients are nicely incorporated, about 4 - 5 minutes. Add black pepper and taste for seasoning. Dip can be served warm or cold.

Store leftover dip in an airtight container with a fitted lid in the fridge for 5 – 7 days.

Pumpkin Seed Pesto

I like using this pesto as a dip, as a spread or poured over noodles. It's diary-free and using pumpkin seeds as the base makes it nut-free too.

Makes about 1 cup

Ingredients:
4 garlic cloves
1/2 cup raw pumpkin seeds
2 cups (packed) fresh basil
1/4 cup lemon juice
1/2 teaspoon sea salt
Pinch black pepper
1/2 cup olive oil

Directions:
Place garlic cloves into a food processor and pulse for 2 - 3 seconds to start breaking them up. Now add the pumpkin seeds, basil, lemon juice, sea salt and black pepper. Start the food processor and while it is running begin pouring in the olive oil in a steady stream. Continue until all of the oil has been added and everything is fully incorporated. Taste for seasoning.

Use immediately or store in an airtight container in the fridge for up to 1 week or in the freezer for up to 1 month.

Herbed "Cheese" Dip

This dip is delicious served with veggies, seeded crackers or on top of soup and chili.

Makes about 2 cups

Ingredients:
1/3 cup filtered water, more if needed
Juice of 1 large or 2 small lemons (about 2 - 3 Tablespoons)
1 Tablespoon apple cider vinegar
3/4 cup raw, unsalted sunflower seeds
1/3 cup raw macadamia nuts
2 medium size garlic cloves
1/4 teaspoon sea salt
Pinch of black pepper
1 - 2 teaspoons of fresh or dried herb of choice, such as cilantro, dill, green onions, or parsley

Directions:
Place all ingredients (except for the herb of your choice) into blender, liquids first. DO NOT add the herb at this time as it will turn the whole dip green! Starting on a low speed, start to blend and then slowly increase to a high speed. You may need to stop and scrape down the sides occasionally. If the dip appears very chunky and has a hard time blending, add 1 Tablespoon of filtered water at a time and then continue blending until the dip is smooth and creamy.

Lastly, add your herb of choice and blend again at a low speed for about 3 – 5 seconds to evenly combine.

Store in an airtight container in the fridge for 5 - 7 days.

*

Homemade Mayonnaise

This recipe works best in a blender that you can manually adjust the speed. Starting at a low speed and slowly moving up to a higher speed while adding in the oil is what gives the mayonnaise its thick and fluffy texture.

Makes about 1 and 1/2 cups

Ingredients:
2 pasteurized eggs*
1/4 teaspoon sea salt
2 teaspoons mustard (recommended brand: Eden Organic Brown Mustard)
1 Tablespoon apple cider vinegar
1 Tablespoon fresh lemon juice
1 cup olive or avocado oil

Directions:
In a dry blender, add the eggs, sea salt, mustard, and vinegar. Set to the lowest speed and blend. While blending, gradually drizzle in the olive oil.

Store in an airtight container with a fitted lid and keep in the fridge for up to two weeks.

If you cannot find pasteurized eggs, here is how to make them at home:
Use fresh, room temperature eggs. If stored in the refrigerator, remove eggs from refrigerator and leave out until they reach room temperature.

Place eggs in a small to medium size saucepan filled with cool water. The water should cover the eggs by 1 inch, and the eggs should not be stacked on top of each other. Place a digital thermometer in the water, hooking it on the lip of the saucepan. This is important for water temperature accuracy!

Place the saucepan over medium heat and slowly bring the water to 140 degrees F. If using large eggs, keep the eggs at this temperature for 3 minutes before removing from water with a slotted spoon. If using extra-large eggs, keep them in the water for 5 minutes before removing them. Do not let the water temperature reach above 142 degrees F. Run the eggs under cold water or give them an ice bath until they return to room temperature. Use eggs right away or store in the fridge for up to 1 week.

Zesty "Ranch" Dip or Dressing

I typically serve this as a dip with flaxseed crackers or sliced vegetables. It's tangy, herby and high in protein. For a salad dressing, drizzle it over crisp romaine lettuce, crunchy cucumbers and sweet cherry tomatoes.

Makes about 1 cup

Ingredients:

1 cup raw hemp seeds
1/4 cup filtered water, more if needed
1/4 cup lemon juice
2 Tablespoons olive oil
3 garlic cloves
1/4 teaspoon sea salt
Pinch black pepper
1 Tablespoon fresh cilantro, minced
1 Tablespoon fresh dill, minced
1 Tablespoon green onions (green part only), minced

Directions:

Carefully rinse hemp seeds under cool water in a fine mesh strainer to remove any dust or dirt. Add rinsed seeds to a blender with the remaining ingredients, except for the cilantro, dill and green onions, as it will turn the whole dip green!

*

Start blending on low speed and gradually increase to high speed, scraping down the sides as necessary. Blend until smooth and creamy, adding a little water if the mixture is too thick and isn't blending well.

Now add the dill and green onions. Return the speed back down to low and blend again for another 2 - 3 seconds. Taste for seasoning and add more sea salt if necessary.

Store leftover dip in an airtight container in the fridge for 7 – 10 days.

Caesar Salad Dressing

I'm in love with this healthier spin on Caesar salad dressing. It's rich and salty with a garlicy bite.

Makes about 1 cup

Ingredients:
1/4 cup filtered water
3 Tablespoons olive oil
3 Tablespoons creamy, unsalted almond or tahini butter
1 Tablespoon apple cider vinegar
Juice of 1 large or 2 small lemons (about 2 Tablespoons)
3 garlic cloves
1/8 teaspoon sea salt

Directions:
Place all ingredients into a blender and starting on a low speed, blend slowly, working up to a high speed. You may have to stop blending a couple of times to scrape down the sides of the blender. Continue blending until creamy. Taste for seasoning and add more sea salt if desired.

Store dressing in an airtight container in the refrigerator for 7 – 10 days, or up to 1 month in the freezer.

Tahini or Almond Butter Drizzle

Tahini is a creamy seed butter made from sesame seeds. It's rich in magnesium, iron and calcium, making it a great choice for dressings and spreads.

Makes about 1/2 cup

Ingredients:
1/2 cup raw tahini or almond butter, unsalted
1/2 cup filtered water
2 Tablespoons fresh lemon juice
2 - 4 drops liquid stevia
2 garlic cloves, smashed and minced
1/4 heaping teaspoon sea salt
Pinch black pepper

DIRECTIONS:
Place all ingredients into a mixing bowl and whisk with a fork to combine. Store leftover drizzle in an airtight container in the fridge for 7 – 10 days.

Traditional Italian Salad Dressing

Tasty salad dressings are so incredibly easy to make at home. You'll never go back to store bought again.

Makes about 1 cup

Ingredients:
1/2 cup olive oil
1/4 cup apple cider vinegar
2 Tablespoons filtered water
1 Tablespoon lemon juice
1/4 teaspoon sea salt
Pinch black pepper
Pinch dried thyme, dill and dried basil (optional)
2 - 3 drops liquid stevia

Directions:
Place all ingredients in a glass mason jar, cover with a fitted lid, and shake well. Dancing while shaking is encouraged. Store dressing in sealed container in the fridge for up to 2 weeks.

Lemon Vinaigrette Dressing

This is my go-to salad dressing most days of the week.

Makes about 1/2 cup

Ingredients:

1/4 cup olive oil
Juice of 1 large or 2 small lemons (about 2 Tablespoons)
2 Tablespoons apple cider vinegar
Pinch sea salt

Directions:

Place all ingredients in a glass mason jar, cover with a fitted lid and shake well.

Store dressing in sealed container in the fridge for up to 2 weeks.

Spicy Mayo Dipping Sauce

Sauces and dips are a great way to keep meals and snacks interesting. I particularly like this dipping sauce served with Crispy Cauliflower.

Makes about 1 cup

Ingredients:

1/3 cup ***Homemade Mayonnaise (see recipe)***
1/4 teaspoon cayenne pepper or hot sauce
¼ teaspoon smoked paprika
1 Tablespoon lemon juice
1 teaspoon brown rice vinegar
2 drops liquid stevia

Directions:

Place all ingredients in a small bowl and using a whisk, mix until fully combined. Store in an airtight container with a fitted lid and keep in the fridge for up to two weeks.

Breads & Desserts

"I totally regret eating healthy today"

- *Said no-one ever*

Garlic, Rosemary Paleo Bread

This bread is dense and hearty and makes the perfect snack. Personally, I love to smear it with grass-fed butter and serve it with Creamy Carrot, Ginger Soup.

Makes 1 loaf

Ingredients:
Coconut or olive oil spray
1 cup almond meal
1/2 cup coconut flour
1/2 cup ground flaxseed meal
1 teaspoon sea salt
1/2 teaspoon baking soda
1 Tablespoon fresh rosemary, minced
6 - 8 cloves fresh garlic, minced
5 eggs
1/2 cup olive oil
1 Tablespoon apple cider vinegar

*

Directions:
Place oven rack in the middle position. Preheat oven to 350 degrees F. and generously grease a loaf pan with oil spray.

In a large mixing bowl, mix together almond meal, coconut flour, ground flaxseed meal, sea salt, baking soda, rosemary, and garlic using a whisk. In a separate bowl whisk together the eggs, olive oil, and apple cider vinegar. Using a wooden spoon, mix the wet ingredients into the dry ingredients until well combined.

Spread the batter (this batter will be thick) into the greased loaf pan, sprinkle a small amount of sea salt over the top (optional), and place in the oven. Bake for about 40 – 50 minutes, or until loaf is firm to the touch and golden brown on top.

Remove from the oven and let cool for about 5 – 10 minutes before removing from loaf pan. Finish cooling on a cooling rack…or slice and enjoy!

This bread should be stored in the fridge and will last for about 5 – 7 days or can be pre-sliced and stored in the freezer for up to a month.

Cassava Tortillas

This soft and chewy tortilla is grain free, but you'd never know it. It looks, feels and taste like a traditional flour tortilla. I like serving them with scrambled eggs, salmon salad, kale sautés or smeared with tahini butter.

Makes 10 – 12 tortillas

Ingredients:
1 cup cassava flour*
1/2 teaspoon sea salt
2/3 cup filtered water, room temperature
2 Tablespoons olive oil

Directions:
Using a whisk, combine the cassava flour and sea salt in a medium sized mixing bowl. Add the water and olive oil, switch to a spoon or mini spatula and combine fully. The batter should not be too wet or too dry and should stick together if you pinch it. If too wet, add more flour 1 Tablespoon at a time. If too dry, add more water, 1 Tablespoon at a time.

Roll all of the batter into balls of about 1 Tablespoon worth, about the size of a golf ball.

If using a tortilla press, line it with 2 pieces of parchment or wax paper, place dough in the center, one ball at a time, and press. If you do not have a tortilla press, you can use 2 pieces of parchment paper and place the batter in the middle and roll out using a rolling pin.

Heat a dry skillet over medium-high heat. Place pressed tortilla on the hot skillet and allow to cook for about 30 seconds, flip over, and cook for 30 seconds more. Cool on a cooling rack. Continue until all the batter is gone.

Enjoy warm. Store leftover tortillas, once completely cooled, in a sealed zip lock bag or container in the fridge. Reheat the same way you made them.

I prefer Otto's brand of Cassava flour. Different brands may require more or less water.

Carrot Muffins

These muffins are soft, moist and just sweet enough. My husband always says you can't have just one.

Makes 12 muffins

Ingredients:

Dry:

1 cup brown rice flour
1/2 cup tapioca flour
1/3 cup xylitol
2 teaspoons cinnamon
1 teaspoon baking soda
3/4 teaspoon xanthan gum
1/2 teaspoon nutmeg
1/2 teaspoon sea salt

Wet:

1/2 cup unsweetened apple sauce
1/3 cup avocado or grape seed oil
3 large eggs
1 dropper full of liquid stevia (about 20 drops, optional)

Fold-ins:

1 and 1/2 cups shredded carrot
1/2 cup chopped walnuts (optional)

Directions:

Preheat oven to 375 degrees F. and place oven rack in the center of the oven. Line a 12-cup muffin tin.

In a large mixing bowl whisk together the dry ingredients. In a separate bowl combine the wet ingredients. Pour the wet ingredients into the dry ingredients and use a wooden spoon to mix everything together. Fold in the shredded carrots and walnuts (if using).

Bake for 25 – 30 minutes, or until a toothpick comes out of the center of a muffin clean.

Store in an airtight container on the counter for 3 days or in the fridge for up to 5 – 7 days.

Blueberry Muffins

Since a candida diet can sometimes feel isolating, it's nice to have classic recipes like blueberry muffins. This recipe also freezes well.

Makes 12 muffins

Ingredients:
3/4 cup plus 2 Tablespoons tapioca starch/flour
1 cup plus 2 Tablespoons brown rice flour
1/3 cup xylitol
2 Tablespoons lemon zest. optional
2 teaspoons baking powder
1 teaspoon xanthan gum
1/2 teaspoon sea salt
1/2 cup coconut oil or grass-fed butter, melted
2 eggs
1/2 cup unsweetened almond or coconut milk
1 cup fresh blueberries

Directions:
Preheat oven to 375 degrees F. and line 12 muffin cups.

In a large mixing bowl combine tapioca starch, brown rice flour, xylitol, lemon zest (if using), baking powder, xanthan gum, and sea salt. Whisk to remove any lumps and evenly combine.

If your coconut oil is in solid form, place 1/2 cup in a small saucepan and bring to a liquid form over low heat.

In a small mixing bowl, beat the eggs, add the almond or coconut milk and while whisking slowly, add the liquid coconut oil. Pour this mixture into the large bowl with the dry ingredients. Switch to a large wooden mixing spoon and stir until everything is evenly combined, being careful not to over-mix. Finally, fold in the fresh blueberries. This batter will be on the thick side.

Scoop about 1/3 cup of batter into each muffin cup and bake for 10 minutes. Rotate the pan and bake another 8 - 10 minutes more, or until golden brown. Let cool for 2 - 3 minutes before removing from muffin tin and transferring to cooling rack.

Blueberry Muffins should be stored in a sealed container in the fridge for up to 1 week.

Rustic Vanilla Scones

These scones are rich and buttery with a golden-brown top. I've made them so many times that I could probably make them in my sleep. I like them as is or served with tahini butter.

Makes 8 - 10 scones

Ingredients:
1/2 cup (1 stick) cold, grass-fed butter
Coconut oil spray
1 cup brown rice flour
3/4 cup tapioca starch/flour or arrowroot
1/3 cup xylitol, more for dusting
2 teaspoons baking powder
1/2 teaspoon xanthan gum
1/2 teaspoon salt
2 large eggs
1/3 cup cold, unsweetened vanilla almond or coconut milk
1 Tablespoon gluten-free vanilla extract

Directions:
Cut the cold butter into small cubes, place on a small plate, and place in the freezer for about 15 minutes to harden. Meanwhile, preheat oven to 400 degrees F. Line a large baking sheet with parchment paper and spray with coconut oil spray. Set aside.

Place the brown rice flour, tapioca flour or arrowroot, xylitol, baking powder, xanthan gum and sea salt into a food processor. Pulse about 2 times to mix dry ingredients. Remove the butter from the freezer and add to the dry ingredients in the food processor. Pulse 5 - 10 times to slightly incorporate the butter.

In a small mixing bowl, whisk together the eggs, milk, and vanilla extract. Add to the food processor and pulse a few times. The dough should be cohesive and very sticky with bits of pea-size butter remaining intact. Place dough into a mixing bowl, cover with plastic wrap and place in the fridge, covered, for about 15 minutes to firm slightly.

Next, using a large spoon, scoop out large spoonful's of batter and place onto prepared baking sheet. Don't fuss with shaping them too much; I like this because it keeps them looking rustic. Spray the tops lightly with oil spray and dust with a little sprinkle of xylitol. Bake for about 13 - 15 minutes or until golden brown. Remove from the oven and let rest for 5 minutes on the baking sheet before transferring to a cooling rack or serving.

Serve warm. I like these with tahini butter spread or grass-fed butter! To store, place scones in a sealed container in the fridge for 4 - 5 days.

For blueberry variation fold in 1/3 – 1/2 cup fresh blueberries after the batter has been mixed and before you place it in the fridge.

Rustic Vanilla Scones

Grain-Free Lemon Scones

For those that don't tolerate grains well, these lemon scones are for you. Using almond flour, which is much softer than almond meal, helps keeps these scones soft and airy.

Makes 6 - 8 scones

Ingredients:
Coconut oil spray
1 cup almond flour (not almond meal)
3/4 cup tapioca starch/flour, more for dusting
1/4 cup coconut flour
1/4 cup xylitol, more for dusting
1/2 teaspoon baking soda
1/2 teaspoon sea salt
2 Tablespoons lemon zest
6 Tablespoons unsalted grass-fed butter, cold, and cut into small cubes
1 large egg
1/4 cup lemon juice
2 Tablespoons unsweetened coconut milk

Directions:
Preheat oven to 350 degrees F. and line a baking sheet with parchment paper and spray lightly with coconut oil spray. In a food processor add the almond flour, tapioca flour, coconut flour, xylitol, baking soda, sea salt and lemon zest. Pulse a couple times to combine. Next, add the cold, cubed butter and pulse a couple more times to break up the butter. At this point the flour should have a consistency similar to wet sand.

In a separate bowl, combine the egg, lemon juice and coconut milk. Pour this into the food processor and process until fully combined.

Lightly flour a working surface with tapioca flour and place the batter in the center. Create a log of about 8 – 10 inches long and 2 inches tall. Cut into 6 – 8 triangle wedges. Place wedges on the prepared baking sheet, spray the top of each scone lightly with coconut oil spray and dust with xylitol. Bake for about 10 – 12 minutes, or until golden brown.

Store leftover scones in an airtight container with a fitted lid in the fridge for 5 – 7 days.

Gluten-Free Pumpkin Scones

These are my favorite scones period!! Starting in October, I'll make a batch almost every single week until I can no longer find pumpkin. Topping them with a powdered xylitol glaze is next level. These scones are insanely delicious.

Makes 8 - 10 scones

Ingredients:

6 Tablespoons unsalted, cold grass-fed butter
Coconut or olive oil spray

Wet:
1/4 cup coconut milk
1/3 cup pumpkin puree
1 Tablespoon apple cider vinegar

Dry:
1 cup brown rice flour
1/2 cup tapioca starch/flour or arrowroot, more for rolling
1/4 cup xylitol, more to sprinkle on top
1 and 1/4 teaspoon baking powder
1 teaspoon ground cinnamon
1/2 teaspoon sea salt
1/2 teaspoon xanthan gum
1/2 teaspoon baking soda
Generous pinch of cloves and nutmeg (optional)

Directions:

Cut the cold butter into small cubes, place on a small dish, and place in the freezer for about 15 minutes to harden. Meanwhile, preheat oven to 400 degrees F. Line a large baking sheet with parchment paper and spray with olive or coconut oil spray. Set aside.

In a small mixing bowl, whisk together the wet ingredients and set aside.

Place all the dry ingredients into a food processor. Pulse about 2 - 3 times to mix. Remove the butter from the freezer and add to the dry ingredients in the food processor. Pulse 5 - 10 times to incorporate the butter into small pieces. Add the wet ingredients and pulse again until the dough is just combined.

Spread a small amount of arrowroot or tapioca flour onto a clean surface and place the dough onto the middle. Carefully roll the dough into a log of about 9 – 10 inches long and 3 - 4 inches wide. Lightly spray the blade of a large knife and also the top of the log with oil spray. Cut the log into 6 rectangles. Place the rectangles on prepared baking sheet and separate each by a few inches to allow room to rise. Dust the tops of each scone with more xylitol.

Bake for about 14 - 16 minutes or until golden brown. Remove from the oven and let rest for 5 minutes on the baking sheet before transferring to a cooling rack. Store leftover scones in a sealed, airtight container in the fridge for 5 – 7 days.

I like to drizzle with Powdered Xylitol Glaze.

Gluten-Free Pumpkin Scones

Powdered Xylitol Glaze

This powdered xylitol glaze is such a treat. I love it drizzled on scones and cookies.

Makes 2 servings

Ingredients:
1/4 cup powdered xylitol*
1 - 2 teaspoons coconut milk
Pinch sea salt

Directions:
Place everything into a small dish and stir until a paste is formed. If the texture is too thin add more powdered xylitol. If it is too thick, add more coconut milk, one drop at a time.

To make powdered xylitol, place xylitol into a spice grinder and pulse for a couple seconds. If you don't have a spice grinder, you could achieve the same results in a dry blender.

Lemon Bars

These Lemon Bars are tangy, decadent and sweet. With a gluten-free crust and a soft, lemony filling, they're proof that being on a specialty diet does not equal boring or tasteless!

Makes about 12 bars

Ingredients:

Coconut oil spray

For the Crust:

3/4 cup brown rice flour
1/4 cup tapioca starch/flour
1 Tablespoon xylitol
1/2 teaspoon xanthan gum
1/2 teaspoon sea salt (if your butter is salted, omit this)
1 stick (or 8 Tablespoons) unsalted, grass-fed butter (cold)
2 – 4 Tablespoons filtered water

For the Filling:

3/4 cup xylitol
1/4 cup freshly squeezed lemon juice
3 Tablespoons arrowroot or tapioca starch/flour
3 large eggs
1 dropper full liquid stevia
Zest of one organic lemon
Generous pinch sea salt

Directions:

Preheat oven to 350 degrees F. and place baking rack on the middle shelf. Grease an eight-inch baking dish by spraying with coconut oil spray.

For the crust, add the brown rice flour, tapioca starch, xylitol, xanthan gum and sea salt (if using) into a food processor and pulse a couple of times. Cut the butter into small cubes and add to the food processor. Pulse again until no large pieces of butter remain. Finally, add filtered water starting with 2 Tablespoons until all the dough comes together.

Pull the dough out of the food processor and place into your prepared baking dish. Dampen your hands with water and then spread the dough evenly on the bottom of the baking dish with your fingers. Using a fork, poke several holes in the crust to prevent air bubbles. Bake for about 35 – 40 minutes, or until golden brown.

In the meantime, prepare the filling by combining all of the filling ingredients in a medium size mixing bowl and whisk until fully combined. Once the crust has finished baking, pour the filling on top of the crust and return to the oven to bake for another 20 – 30 minutes, or until filling is set and does not jiggle.

Remove from oven and place on a wire rack to cool. Chill bars for about 2 - 3 hours in the refrigerator before cutting. Store bars in an airtight container in the fridge for 5 – 7 days.

Lemon Bars

Ginger Spiced Cookies

These cookies are soft and chewy with a kick of ginger. If you have the time, I highly recommend using fresh ginger juice as it really makes the flavor pop.

Makes 9 large or 12 small cookies

Ingredients:
1/2 cup creamy, unsalted almond butter
1 large egg
1/2 cup shredded coconut
1/3 cup xylitol
1 teaspoon ground cinnamon
1 teaspoon ground ginger powder*
1/2 teaspoon baking soda
1/4 teaspoon sea salt

Directions:
In a large mixing bowl, place the almond butter and egg and use a fork to whisk together until fully combined. In a separate bowl whisk together the shredded coconut, xylitol, cinnamon, ginger powder, baking soda and sea salt. Add the wet ingredients to the dry ingredients and using a large wooden spoon mix until fully combined. Wrap in plastic wrap and place in the fridge for about 15 minutes to set.

Preheat oven to 350 degrees F. and line a baking sheet with parchment paper.

Remove the batter from the fridge and place 1 – 2 Tablespoons at a time onto the baking sheet, leaving 2 - 3 inches in between so the cookies can spread out. Bake for 10 – 12 minutes, or until the cookies turn golden brown. Remove from oven and let cool for 5 minutes on baking sheet before transferring to a cooling rack.

Store leftover cookies in the fridge in a sealed container for up to 1 week or in the freezer for up to 1 month.

Option to substitute fresh ginger juice by grating a piece of freshly peeled ginger on a microplane or fine grater and then bunching the gratings together and squeezing them over a fine mesh strainer into the almond butter/egg mixture. Ginger must be extremely fresh in order to extract juice.

Grain-Free "Shortbread" Cookies

These are the perfect cookies for when you're looking for something that's not overly sweet to snack on.

Makes about 14 - 16 cookies

Ingredients:
3/4 cup almond meal or flour
1/3 cup xylitol
1/4 cup coconut flour
1/4 cup shredded coconut
1/2 teaspoon baking soda
1/4 teaspoon sea salt
2 eggs
2 Tablespoons creamy, unsalted almond, pecan or walnut butter
1 Tablespoon coconut oil, melted
1 Tablespoon vanilla extract
10 drops liquid stevia

Directions:
Preheat oven to 350 degrees F. and line a baking sheet with parchment paper.

In a large mixing bowl whisk together the almond flour, xylitol, coconut flour, shredded coconut, baking soda, and sea salt.

In a smaller mixing bowl whisk together the eggs, nut butter, coconut oil, vanilla extract, and liquid stevia.

Add the wet ingredients to the dry ingredients and use a spatula to combine.

Scoop about 1 Tablespoon at a time onto the baking sheet (they won't spread much so you don't need to worry about leaving a lot of space in between them). Bake for 6 minutes, rotate the pan and bake for 6 – 10 minutes more, or until golden brown.

Store leftover cookies in an airtight container with a fitted lid in the fridge for 5 – 7 days or in the freezer for up to 1 month.

Almond Butter Cookies

The strawberries in these cookies are a unique twist making them light, slightly sweet and elegant.

Makes about 12 large cookies

Ingredients:
Coconut or olive oil spray for baking sheet
1/3 cup xylitol
2 Tablespoons unsweetened shredded coconut
1/2 teaspoon baking soda
1/2 teaspoon cinnamon
1/2 teaspoon sea salt
1 cup creamy, unsalted almond butter
3 Tablespoons of non-dairy, unsweetened almond or coconut milk, more if needed
1 large egg, beaten
1/2 cup fresh strawberries, chopped OR Cacao paste or nibs

Directions:
Line a baking sheet with parchment paper and spray lightly with coconut or olive oil spray. Set aside.

In a medium-sized mixing bowl whisk together the xylitol, shredded coconut, baking soda, cinnamon, and sea salt. In a separate bowl, combine the almond butter, non-dairy milk, and egg. Add the almond butter mixture to the dry ingredients and using a wooden spoon, mix everything together until fully combined. If it's difficult to mix because the batter is too thick, add another tablespoon of non-dairy milk.

Fold in the strawberries and place in the fridge to set for about 10 minutes.

Set the oven to 350 degrees F. and place the oven rack on the middle shelf. Scoop about 2 Tablespoons* worth of batter onto the prepared baking sheet and press down gently in the middle. Bake for about 8 – 10 minutes, or until almost firm to touch. Let cool on the baking sheet for about 5 minutes before transferring to cooling rack and cooling completely.

Store leftover cookies in the fridge in a sealed container for up to 1 week or in the freezer for up to 1 month.

For smaller cookies, reduce to 1 Tablespoon of batter per cookie. This should yield around 24 small cookies.

Lemon, Poppy Seed Cookies

Lemon cookies are a nice change of pace from the typical chocolate dessert. The combination of lemon and poppyseeds go together like peanut butter and jelly. These cookies are soft, spongy and perfectly sweet. They also freeze well.

Makes about 12 – 14 Cookies

Ingredients:

3/4 cup almond, pecan or hazelnut meal*
1/4 cup tapioca starch/flour
3 Tablespoons shredded unsweetened coconut
2 Tablespoons coconut flour
1/2 teaspoon baking powder
1/4 teaspoon sea salt
1/4 cup poppy seeds
1/4 cup xylitol
2 large eggs
2 Tablespoons coconut oil, melted
1/2 teaspoon vanilla extract
1/8 teaspoon almond extract (optional)
10 drops liquid stevia
1 Tablespoon lemon juice and zest

Directions:

In a large mixing bowl combine the almond meal, tapioca starch, shredded coconut, coconut flour, baking powder, sea salt, poppy seeds, and xylitol. In a separate bowl combine the eggs, oil, vanilla, almond extract (if using), liquid stevia, lemon zest and juice. Add the wet ingredients into the dry ingredients and using a wooden spoon, stir to combine.

Cover mixing bowl with plastic wrap and chill batter in the fridge for a least 30 minutes, or until it firms up a bit.

Preheat oven to 325 degrees F. and line a baking sheet with parchment paper.

Spoon onto baking sheet about 1 heaping Tablespoon at a time. Bake for 10 – 12 minutes, or until golden brown. Let cookies sit on baking sheet for 5 minutes before moving to a cooling rack. Store leftover cookies in an airtight container with a fitted lid in the fridge for 5 – 7 days or in the freezer for up to 1 month.

***To make your own almond, pecan or hazelnut meal simply place raw, dry and unsalted nuts in a food processor and pulse until a meal is created.**

I like to drizzle with Powdered Xylitol Glaze.

Cacao Chip Cookies

A candida friendly take on the classic chocolate chip cookie. Sans the gluten and the sugar.

Makes about 12 cookies

Ingredients:

Oil spray (coconut or olive oil spray work well)
1 stick (8 Tablespoons) grass-fed butter, unsalted, and room temperature
6 Tablespoons xylitol
1 large egg
1 dropper full liquid stevia
1/2 cup plus 3 Tablespoons tapioca flour
1/2 cup brown rice flour
1/2 teaspoon baking soda
1/2 teaspoon ground cinnamon
1/2 teaspoon sea salt
1/2 teaspoon xanthan gum
1/3 cup chopped cacao paste or stevia sweetened chocolate chips*

Directions:

Preheat oven to 350 degrees F. and line a baking sheet with parchment paper. Spray lightly with oil spray. Set aside. In a large mixing bowl cream together the butter and xylitol. Do this either with a mixer or manually mash them together into a paste with a spoon or spatula. Add the egg and liquid stevia and mix together.

In a separate bowl combine the tapioca flour, brown rice flour, baking soda, ground cinnamon, sea salt, and xanthan gum. Add this to the bowl with the butter and use a wooden spoon or spatula to mix until fully combined. This dough will be on the thick side. Fold in the chopped cacao paste or chocolate chips.

Scoop onto prepared baking sheet about 1 heaping Tablespoon at a time, leaving about 2 – 3 inches between each cookie. Bake for 8 – 10 minutes, or until golden brown. Cookies will be solid on the outside but soft on the inside. Let cool for 5 minutes on baking sheet before transferring to cooling rack.

Store leftover cookies in an airtight container with a fitted lid in the fridge for 5 – 7 days or in the freezer for up to 1 month.

Lily's Brand sells a chocolate chip that is sweetened with stevia. However, they contain soy and corn so it's best to use them only on special occasions.

Pumpkin, Cacao Chip Cookies

These Pumpkin, Cacao Chip Cookies are a real treat. They're soft and fudgy, and I enjoy them straight from the fridge. Baker beware, I bet you can't eat just one. ☺

Makes about 12 cookies

Ingredients:

Dry:
5 Tablespoons coconut flour
1/4 cup arrowroot or tapioca flour
1/4 cup xylitol
1/2 teaspoon baking soda
1/2 teaspoon ground cinnamon
1/4 teaspoon xanthan gum
1/4 teaspoon sea salt

Wet:
1/3 cup organic pumpkin puree, canned
2 Tablespoons grass-fed butter or coconut oil, melted
1 large egg
10 drops liquid stevia

Fold in:
1/4 cup chopped cacao paste or cacao nibs

Directions:
In a medium sized mixing bowl whisk together the dry ingredients. In a separate bowl whisk together the wet.

Pour the wet ingredients into the dry mixture and using a spatula or wooden spoon mix to combine. Fold in the chopped cacao paste. Cover the bowl with plastic wrap and place in the fridge to chill for about 30 minutes.

Preheat oven to 350 degrees F. and line a baking sheet with parchment paper. Spray lightly with oil. Scoop about 2 heaping Tablespoons of batter at a time and form into a ball with your hands. Place on prepared baking sheet and flatten slightly with your hands. These cookies will not spread.

Bake for 8 – 10 minutes. Let cool and enjoy. I find that these are best stored and enjoyed straight from the fridge.

****Lily's dark chocolate chips are an occasional option to substitute for the cacao paste.***

Chocolate Pudding

Full fat coconut cream gives this pudding its thick, decadent and creamy texture.

Make 2 – 4 servings

Ingredients:
1 (13.5-ounce) can full-fat coconut cream*
1/4 cup unsweetened cocoa powder
1 Tablespoon xylitol
10 drops liquid stevia
Pinch sea salt
Toppings: unsweetened shredded coconut, slivered almonds, cacao nibs

Directions:
Place all ingredients into a blender and starting on low speed, blend slowly working up to high speed. Blend until smooth and creamy, scrapping down the sides as necessary. Enjoy with additional toppings.

Store in a mason jar or an airtight container with a fitted lid in the fridge for 5 – 7 days.

Do NOT use Trader Joe's brand for this recipe. They have reformulated their coconut cream and it is now too watery and clumpy and does not work well.

Saucy Mixed Berries

Saucy berries are delicious enjoyed as-is or added to granola or on top of pancakes.

Makes 6 servings

Ingredients:
Filling:
1 (16-ounce) bag frozen* mixed berries** (about 2 - 3 cups)
1 Tablespoon tapioca starch diluted in 2 Tablespoons filtered water
Pinch sea salt

Directions:
Preheat oven to 350 degrees F.

Place all the filling ingredients into an 8 x 8 baking dish or pie dish. Using your hands mix everything together. Cover with foil.

Bake for about 20 – 25 minutes, until the fruit is bubbling.

Store in an airtight container in the refrigerator for 4 – 5 days.

If using fresh berries, reduce cooking time by about 5 minutes.
*****Ensure that the mixed berries contain no cherries for the Anti-Candida diet.***

Option to create a Berry Crumble by adding Nutty Power Granola or Vanilla Granola when serving!

Pumpkin Pie

I created this recipe because the holidays can be a big source of stress for those following a candida diet. In fact, one of the most frequent questions I get asked is how to survive the holidays. Rest assured that you now have this sugar-free pumpkin pie recipe to help.

Makes 1 pie

Ingredients:

Crust:

Coconut oil spray
1 cup, plus 2 Tablespoons, brown rice flour
1/4 cup, plus 2 Tablespoons tapioca starch/flour, more for flouring
1 Tablespoon xylitol
3/4 teaspoon xanthan gum
3/4 teaspoon sea salt (if your butter is salted, omit this)
1 and 1/2 sticks (or 12 Tablespoons) unsalted, grass-fed butter (cold)
4 - 6 Tablespoons filtered water

Filling:

1 (15-ounce) can pumpkin puree
1 cup full fat coconut milk*
2 large eggs
1/3 cup xylitol
2 teaspoons cinnamon
1/2 teaspoon ground ginger
1/2 teaspoon sea salt
1/4 teaspoon ground nutmeg
20 drops liquid stevia

Directions:

Preheat oven to 350 degrees F. and place baking rack on the middle shelf. Grease a standard, 9-inch pie dish with coconut oil spray.

For the crust, add the brown rice flour, tapioca starch, xylitol, xanthan gum and sea salt (if using) to a food processor. Pulse a couple times to combine. Cut the butter into small cubes, add to the food processor and pulse again until no large pieces of butter remain. Finally, add the filtered water, starting with 2 Tablespoons, until all the dough comes together.

Pull the dough out of the food processor and place into your prepared pie dish. Start to press the dough into the pie dish and then lightly dust it with tapioca starch and continue to spread the dough evenly on the bottom and up the sides of the dish with your fingers. Using a fork, poke several holes throughout the crust.

Bake for 20 minutes. Remove from oven and let cool for just a few minutes while creating the filling.

Place the pie dish on a baking sheet (this will catch any filling that might spill over). Place all the filling ingredients into a blender and blend until smooth and creamy. Add the filling to the piecrust and carefully place in oven. Bake for about 50 – 60 minutes more, or until a toothpick stuck into the pie about an inch from the edge of the crust comes out clean.

Remove from oven and let cool for about 20 minutes before transferring to the fridge to finish setting, uncovered, for at least 2 hours before serving.

Store leftover pie in the fridge for up to 5 – 7 days.

****Canned, full fat coconut milk is best since it's thicker.***

Pumpkin Pie

Homemade Almond Meal

Now that you're turning into a pro in the kitchen, try making your own almond meal. Why throw out your nut milk pulp, when you can make it into a meal that you'll use for baking.

Ingredients:
Almond pulp from making Nut Milk

Directions:
Preheat oven to 250 degrees F. and line a baking sheet with parchment paper.

Spread the wet pulp on the baking sheet in an even layer. Place in the oven for 60 – 90 minutes, removing and gently stirring every 30 minutes. Continue until the pulp is dry.

Place dried pulp into a dry blender for traditional almond meal, or a coffee grinder for almond flour.

Store leftover almond meal or flour in an airtight container with a fitted lid or a zip lock back in the fridge for 3 – 4 weeks for in the freezer for up to 3 months.

Optional Proteins

"Healthy Habits are learned in the same way as unhealthy ones – through practice."

- *Wayne Dyer*

Baked Salmon, Mahi Mahi or Cod

Makes 2 servings

Ingredients:
1 pound fresh or frozen and defrosted salmon, mahi mahi or cod
1 Tablespoon olive oil
Zest of one lemon
Pinch of sea salt

Directions:
Preheat oven to 350 degrees F. and line a baking sheet with foil or parchment paper.

Place fish skin side down and drizzle with olive oil, lemon zest and sea salt. Bake for about 10 – 12 minutes* or until easily flaked with a fork in the center.

Cooking time will vary depending on the size of your fish.

Baked Chicken

Makes 2 servings

Ingredients:
2 organic, hormone-free chicken breasts, rinsed and patted dry
1 Tablespoon olive oil
Pinch sea salt
Pinch black pepper
Favorite seasoning (optional)

Directions:
Preheat oven to 350 degrees F. and line a baking sheet with parchment paper.

Place chicken breasts on baking sheet. Drizzle with olive oil and sprinkle sea salt, pepper, and any other desired seasoning. Using gloved hands, rub all ingredients into chicken breasts evenly. Bake for about 25 - 35 minutes, or until it reaches an internal temperature of 165 F. (at the thickest part) and is opaque all the way through.

Perfect Hard-Boiled Eggs

Ingredients:
Large eggs, preferably Certified Organic
Water

Directions:
Place eggs in a large saucepan and cover with cool water by 1 inch. Eggs should not be stacked on one another. Bring water to a boil over medium-high heat. Once boiling, cover with a fitted lid and turn off the heat. Let sit for 15 minutes.

Transfer eggs to a colander and place under cool running water to stop the cooking. Eggs can be peeled and served immediately.

Eggs Over Easy

Makes 2 servings

Ingredients:
2 Tablespoons olive oil, coconut oil or unsalted grass-fed butter, divided
4 large eggs
Pinch sea salt
Pinch black pepper

Directions:
Heat a medium non-stick skillet over medium-low heat and add 2 Tablespoons of oil or butter. Once the oil is hot, crack the eggs into the pan. Depending on pan size, you may want to do this 2 at a time. Sprinkle eggs with a pinch of sea salt and pepper. Once the whites start to set and go from translucent to white, gently lift one side and flip the egg over, avoiding breaking the yolk. Cook for about 1 minute more.

Slide onto serving plate and enjoy warm.

Foods to Eat & Avoid

"Let food be thy medicine and medicine be thy food."

- Hippocrates

Foods to Eat

BEANS & LEGUMES TO EAT

(Enjoy only 1 - 2 times per week, or avoid until after 30 days)

Adzuki beans	Black beans	Fava Beans	Pinto Beans	Lentils
Garbanzo beans	Kidney beans	Navy Beans	Mung beans	White beans
Lima beans				

CONDIMENTS TO EAT

Apple cider vinegar	Brown rice vinegar	Homemade mayonnaise	Umeboshi vinegar	Coconut aminos
Guacamole	Salsa	Mustard (*made with apple cider vinegar*)		

DAIRY PRODUCTS TO EAT

Unsalted grass-fed butter	Unsweetened non-diary milk *(almond, coconut, hemp)*	Ghee

DRINKS AND MISCELLANEOUS TO EAT AND DRINK

Gum/mints (*xylitol based*)	Mineral water	Teas – green and herbal

FRUITS TO EAT

Green apples	Lemons/limes	Strawberries	Avocados	Coconut
Blueberries	Blackberries	Grapefruit	Raspberries	Cranberries (*fresh, unsweetened*)

GRAINS & FLOURS TO EAT

Amaranth	Tapioca	Buckwheat/flour	Brown rice/flour	Coconut flour
Millet	Arrowroot	Quinoa/flour	Tigernut flour	Cassava flour
Teff/flour	Kuzu or Kudzu root	Wild rice		

MEAT, POULTRY & FISH TO EAT

(free range, hormone free, antibiotic free, grass-fed)

Beef or bison	Lamb	Turkey	Chicken	Salmon
Mahi Mahi	Cod	Shellfish	Egg (*pasture raised*)	

NUTS & SEEDS TO EAT

Almonds	Walnuts	Macadamia nuts	Chestnuts	Hazelnuts
Brazil nuts	Sunflower seeds	Hemp seeds	Pumpkin seeds	Flax seeds
Pecans	Pine nuts	Sesame seeds	Chia seeds	Tiger Nuts

OILS TO EAT

Olive oil	Coconut oil	Safflower oil	Sunflower oil	Grapeseed oil
Walnut oil *(no heat)*	Almond oil *(no heat)*	Hemp seed oil *(no heat)*	Flaxseed oil *(no heat)*	Sesame oil *(no heat)*
Avocado oil				

ORGANIC VEGETABLES TO EAT

Artichoke	Asparagus	Bamboo Shoot	Beets	Broccoli
Brussels Sprouts	Bok Choy	Carrots	Cabbage	Cauliflower
Celery	Chives	Collard greens	Cucumbers	Daikon
Dandelion	Endive	Fennel	Garlic	Kale
Kelp	Leeks	Lettuces	Mustard greens	Sea vegetables
Okra	Olives	Onion	Parsley	Parsnip
Pumpkin	Radish	Rhubarb	Rutabaga	Jicama
Spinach	Zucchini	Yams	Watercress	Water chestnuts
Turnips	Swiss chard	Sweet potatoes	All squash	***Tomatoes****
Eggplant*	***Peppers****			

Eat in moderation or avoid completely if you have arthritis or experience achy joints.

SWEETENERS TO EAT

Pure stevia (*liquid/powder*)	Xylitol (*birch source*)	Luo han (*Monk fruit extract*)	Chicory root

Enjoy after 60 days

Cacao nibs (*unsweetened)* Cacao and Cacao powder (unsweetened) Cacao Paste
Gluten free oats and flour

Enjoy after 90 days

Goat's milk and cheese (raw)* ***Sheep's milk and cheese (raw)****
Pregnant or nursing women should not eat raw dairy products

Apricots	Bananas	Cherries	Guava	Tangerines
Mango	Oranges	Papayas	Pears	Pineapple
Pomegranate	Kiwi	Melons	Peaches	Prunes
Persimmon	Plum			

Pistachios Cashews

Peas/Green beans

Fermented Foods
(*Kimchi, sauerkraut, tempeh, yogurt, nutritional yeast, cultured vegetables*)

Avoid:

BEANS TO AVOID

Tempeh Tofu Soybeans/Soy products

CONDIMENTS TO AVOID

Gravy Relish Jams and jellies Store-bought Ketchup Salad dressing (*store bought*)

Pickles Store-bought Mayo Balsamic vinegar Red wine vinegar Worcestershire sauce

Vinegars (*except apple cider vinegar and brown rice vinegar*)

Soy sauce, ponzu and tamari

Sauces and vinegars with sugar

Spices that contain yeast, sugar or additives

Mustard (*unless made with apple cider vinegar*)

DAIRY TO AVOID

Kefir Ice cream Margarine Yogurt Buttermilk

Cheese Sour cream Cow's milk

FRUITS TO AVOID

Dates Dried fruit Raisins Fruit Juice

GRAINS TO AVOID

Barley White Flours White Rice Rye Whole Wheat/flour

Farro Kamut Spelt Corn Pasta (*except gluten free*)

Breads (*except gluten, dairy, yeast and sugar free*)

Cereals (*except gluten, dairy and sugar free*)

Crackers (*except gluten, dairy, yeast and sugar free*)

MEAT, POULTRY & FISH TO AVOID

Tuna Hotdogs Pork Sausages Bacon (*except turkey*)

Processed and packaged meats

NUTS TO AVOID

Peanuts/Peanut Butter

OILS TO AVOID

Canola oil Corn oil Cottonseed oil Peanut oil Soybean oil

Processed oils and partially hydrogenated and hydrogenated oils

SWEETNERS TO AVOID

Agave nectar	Brown rice syrup	Barley malt	Brown Sugar	All cane sugar or juice
Corn syrup	Maple syrup	Fructose	Honey	Coconut sugar/nectar
Molasses	Yacon syrup	White sugar	Saccharin	

Erythritol (*Truvia, Nectresse, Swerve*)
Aspartame (*nutra sweet*)

VEGETABLES TO AVOID

Corn	Mushrooms	Potatoes

MISCELLANEOUS TO AVOID

Alcohol	Candy/Chocolates	Jell-O	Fast food	Fried food
Gluten	Soda			

Breakfast & Beverages

"No one is born a great cook, one learns by doing."

- *Julia Child*

Almond Milk

This milk alternative is creamy, nutrient rich and ready in minutes. I find almond milk to be the most neutral in flavor of all the non-dairy milks.

Makes 3 – 4 cups

Ingredients:
1 cup raw almonds
4 cups filtered water
Pinch sea salt
1 teaspoon vanilla extract or 1 vanilla bean (optional)
5 – 6 drops liquid stevia (optional)

Directions:
Place almonds into a fine mesh strainer and rinse under cold water to remove any dust or dirt. Next place them into a Vitamix or high-powered blender and add filtered water, sea salt, vanilla, and stevia.

Start blending on low speed, working up to high speed, until you have a creamy consistency. Using a nut milk bag, cheesecloth, or an extremely fine mesh strainer*, strain the pulp out of the milk and discard.**

Store in an airtight glass jar in the refrigerator for up to 3 - 5 days.

If using a fine mesh strainer, you may need to strain several times.
*****Option to make Homemade Almond Meal out of the pulp.***

Brazil Nut Milk

Brazil nuts make this milk thick and rich. They're also high in selenium which is beneficial for thyroid health. I love Brazil Nut Milk poured over nutty granola or warmed up and served in a mug.

Makes 3 – 4 cups

Ingredients:
1 cup raw Brazil nuts
5 cups filtered water
1/4 teaspoon ground cinnamon
Pinch sea salt
1 teaspoon vanilla extract or 1 vanilla bean (optional)
4 – 6 drops liquid stevia (optional)

Directions:
Place Brazil nuts into a fine mesh strainer and rinse under cold water to remove any dust or dirt. Next place them into a Vitamix or high-powered blender and add filtered water, cinnamon, sea salt, vanilla, and liquid stevia.

Start blending on low speed, working up to high speed, until you have a creamy consistency. Using a nut milk bag, cheesecloth, or an extremely fine mesh strainer*, strain the pulp out of the milk and discard.

Store in an airtight glass jar in the refrigerator for up to 3 - 5 days.

If using a fine mesh strainer, you may need to strain several times.

*

Golden Turmeric Milk

This rich and creamy drink helps give your immune system an extra boost. Turmeric is an anti-inflammatory and antioxidant powerhouse. It's also thought to help with brain function and fight off depression, so drink up!

Makes 2 small servings

Ingredients:
1 (13.5-ounce) can full fat coconut milk, or about 1 and 3/4 cups of your favorite unsweetened non-dairy milk
3/4 teaspoon ground ginger OR 1-inch piece fresh ginger, minced
3/4 teaspoon ground turmeric OR 1-inch piece of fresh turmeric, minced
1/4 teaspoon ground cinnamon
1 teaspoon grass-fed butter or coconut oil
2 teaspoons xylitol
Pinch nutmeg
Pinch sea salt
6 - 10 drops liquid stevia

Directions:
If using fresh ginger and turmeric, wash and cut into small pieces. Place milk, fresh or dried turmeric and ginger, and ground cinnamon into a small saucepan and bring to a boil over medium-high heat. Whisk to combine, reduce heat to low, and simmer for about 5 – 10 minutes. Remove from heat and strain through a fine mesh strainer if you are using fresh turmeric and ginger.

Pour strained liquid into a blender with the remaining ingredients. Blend until fully combined and frothy. Enjoy warm.

Store leftover milk in a mason jar with a fitted lid in the fridge for 4 – 5 days.

Enjoy through a straw since turmeric will stain your teeth!

Hot Yerba Mate Latte

Here's a warm and frothy latte recipe that you can indulge in without fear of blowing your candida diet. As a bonus, Yerba mate has anti-inflammatory and antioxidant properties that may help boost your immune system.

Makes 1 large cup

Ingredients:
1 and 1/2 cups filtered water
1/2 cup unsweetened almond, coconut or hemp milk
1 teaspoon coconut oil or unsalted grass-fed butter
1 teaspoon Yerba Mate powder (I prefer Yerba Mate Royale Brand)
1 teaspoon xylitol
4 – 6 drops liquid stevia
1/4 teaspoon ground cinnamon
Pinch sea salt

Directions:
Heat 1 and 1/2 cups of filtered water, non-dairy milk and coconut oil or butter in a small saucepan to almost boiling.

Meanwhile, place the Yerba Mate, xylitol, stevia, cinnamon, and sea salt into a blender. Add heated mixture. Place a dishtowel over the lid to protect your hand from the hot water and start blending at a low speed, gradually increasing to a high speed. Blend for about 30 - 45 seconds or until mixture starts to look frothy.

Pour into your favorite coffee mug.

Note: If you would like a stronger latte, add more yerba mate, 1 teaspoon at a time, during blending. Wisdom of the Ancients Instant Yerba Mate Royale is sweetened with stevia, so there is no need to add more sweetener when using this brand.

*

Gleaming Green Juice

A healthy and hydrating green juice recipe is slightly sweet with a kick of ginger. Green juices are a fast and easy way to absorb nutrients and increase energy levels. They also give your digestive system a little rest while helping your skin to glow.

Makes 1 large serving

Ingredients:
1 organic green apple
1 organic lemon or lime
1 large organic hothouse cucumber
2 ribs organic celery
1 (1-inch) piece organic ginger root
1 bunch organic romaine lettuce
1 small handful organic cilantro

Directions:
Wash all the vegetables in the sink under cool water to remove any dust or debris. Now place them into a high powdered juicer and juice.

Enjoy immediately or store in an airtight glass jar with a fitted lid in the fridge for up to 3 days.

Protein Power Smoothie

The avocado in this recipe might surprise you, but it makes this smoothie thick and rich while adding a serving of healthy fats.

Makes 1 large serving

Ingredients:
1 cup frozen berries
1 cup packed spinach
1 and 1/2 cups unsweetened almond or coconut milk
1/4 ripe avocado
1 Tablespoon flaxseed oil
1 scoop protein powder (hemp or brown rice*)
1 teaspoon Spirulina powder OR 1 scoop Nano greens (optional)

Directions:
Put all the ingredients into a high powdered blender. Starting on low speed, start to blend, slowly working up to high speed. Blend until smooth and creamy.

Enjoy immediately or store in an airtight glass jar with a fitted lid in the fridge for up to 3 days.

Make sure your protein powder has no sugar added.

Strawberries and Cream Smoothie

While the Dragon Fruit powder in this smoothie is optional, it creates this beautiful rose color as shown below while also adding antioxidants and vitamins.

Makes 1 large serving

Ingredients:
1 cup unsweetened coconut milk (can or carton)
1 cup fresh strawberries, stems removed
1 scoop vanilla protein powder (hemp or brown rice*)
1 Tablespoon chia seeds
4 drops liquid stevia
1/4 teaspoon vanilla extract
1/4 teaspoon dragon fruit powder (optional)
Pinch sea salt

Directions:
Put all the ingredients into a high powdered blender. Starting on low speed, start to blend, slowly working up to high speed. Blend until smooth and creamy.

Enjoy immediately or store in an airtight glass jar with a fitted lid in the fridge for up to 3 days.

Make sure your protein powder has no added sugar.

Blueberry, Coconut Quinoa Porridge

Quinoa is typically thought of as a lunch or dinner grain, but I also enjoy it as a breakfast porridge. I like the soft and chewy texture quinoa takes on after being cooked low and slow in non-dairy milk.

Makes 2 - 3 servings

Ingredients:
1 cup uncooked white quinoa
1 cup fresh blueberries, more for garnish
2 - 3 cups unsweetened coconut or almond milk
1 heaping Tablespoon almond butter
2 Tablespoons xylitol
1 teaspoon vanilla extract (no sugar added)
Pinch sea salt

Optional garnish:
Unsweetened shredded coconut
1 heaping Tablespoon coconut cream

Directions:
Thoroughly rinse quinoa in a fine mesh strainer to remove any dust and dirt.

Place quinoa, blueberries, 2 cups coconut or almond milk, almond butter, xylitol, vanilla extract, and a pinch of sea salt in a medium size saucepan and bring to a boil over high heat. Reduce heat to low, cover with a fitted lid, and simmer for about 15 minutes. At this point add more coconut or almond milk if necessary and simmer about 5 minutes more.

Serve warm and garnished with a sprinkle of shredded coconut, a dollop of coconut cream and fresh blueberries.

Cinnamon Spiced Oatmeal

When the mornings get chilly, I switch to creamy cinnamon spiced oats. Cinnamon is a warming spice that lends a sweet flavor and makes the whole house smell irresistible.

Makes 2 large servings

Ingredients:
1 cup gluten-free rolled oats
4 cups unsweetened almond or coconut milk
2 Tablespoons xylitol
1 teaspoon vanilla extract (no sugar added)
Pinch nutmeg (optional)
Pinch sea salt
1 teaspoon ground cinnamon
5 - 10 drops liquid stevia
Slivered almonds for garnish

Directions:
In a large saucepan, combine rolled oats, non-dairy milk, xylitol, vanilla, nutmeg (if using) and sea salt. Bring to a boil. Reduce heat to low, cover and simmer, stirring occasionally until oats are soft and creamy, about 15 minutes. Cooking time may vary depending on the oats you purchase, so also refer to cooking instructions on your oats. When finished cooking, oats should be creamy and thick, but still have some liquid around the edges of the saucepan.

Add cinnamon and 5 - 10 drops of liquid stevia, depending on the desired sweetness, stir to combine, and simmer for about 1 – 2 minutes more.

Taste for seasoning. Serve garnished with a sprinkle of cinnamon and slivered almonds.

Homemade Muesli

Muesli is a breakfast cereal I was introduced to during my travels throughout India. Traditional muesli usually contains dried fruit which I've subbed for fresh fruit to reduce sugar. I like to make a big batch of muesli to always have on hand in a pinch.

Makes about 5 cups

Ingredients:

For dry muesli:
2 cups puffed millet
2 cups quinoa crisps (Nuts.com)*
3/4 cup unsweetened coconut flakes
1/2 cup raw pumpkin seeds
1/2 cup raw sunflower seeds
1/2 teaspoon ground cinnamon
2 pinches sea salt

Additional ingredients when served:
About 1 cup unsweetened almond or coconut milk
1/2 cup fresh berries of choice
Liquid stevia (optional)

Directions:
Add all dry ingredients to a large bowl and stir to combine evenly. Serve 1 cup dry muesli with fresh berries and non-dairy milk of choice. Option to add 2 - 3 drops of liquid stevia to non-dairy milk before adding it to muesli.

Store dry muesli in an airtight container and place in a pantry or other cool, dark place. This should last 3 - 4 weeks.

***You can also sub puffed rice or more puffed millet.**

Lemon-Blueberry Waffles

The combination of lemon and blueberries help give these waffles a nice, light flavor. They're perfect for weekend brunches with family or friends.

Makes 4 – 5 servings

Ingredients:
1 cup brown rice flour
1/4 cup, plus 2 tablespoons, arrowroot or tapioca starch/flour
2 Tablespoons xylitol
1 teaspoon baking powder
1 teaspoon xanthan gum
1/2 teaspoon sea salt
Zest and juice of 1 lemon
1 and 1/4 cups unsweetened coconut or almond milk
2 Tablespoons coconut oil, liquid form
2 eggs
1 dropper full liquid stevia (about 20 drops)
1 cup fresh blueberries
Coconut or olive oil spray

Directions:
Preheat waffle iron.

In a medium-size mixing bowl, whisk together the brown rice flour, arrowroot or tapioca starch, xylitol, baking powder, and sea salt until well combined and free of lumps. Zest the lemon into the bowl by grating the entire yellow surface layer, making sure not to grate into the white rind, which is bitter. Whisk zest into the dry mixture.

In a separate smaller bowl, juice the lemon. Add the non-dairy milk, oil, eggs and liquid stevia. Add the wet ingredients to the dry ingredients and mix until completely combined. Gently fold the blueberries into the mixture.

For each waffle, generously spray the heated waffle iron surface with coconut oil spray. Pour batter, about 1/3 cup at a time, into the center of the waffle iron and cook according to your iron's instructions. When each waffle is done, remove it from the iron (I like to use a fork to carefully pry the waffle out of the iron). Enjoy warm.

I like serving with Lemon, Blueberry Syrup.

Grain-Free Power Waffles

Almond meal makes the base of these grain-free waffles. It's high in protein, low in carbs with a slightly sweet flavor.

Makes 2 – 4 servings

Ingredients:
1 and 1/2 cups almond meal
1/4 cup tapioca starch/flour
2 Tablespoons xylitol
1/2 teaspoon baking powder
1/4 teaspoon baking soda
1/4 teaspoon sea salt
3 eggs
1/3 cup unsweetened coconut or almond milk
3 Tablespoons olive oil or coconut oil, liquid form
2 Tablespoons creamy, unsalted almond butter
1 dropper full liquid stevia (about 20 drops)
1 teaspoon vanilla extract
1/3 cup fresh blueberries
Coconut oil spray

Directions:
Preheat waffle iron.

Combine the almond meal, tapioca starch, xylitol, baking powder, baking soda, and sea salt in a large mixing bowl. In a separate smaller bowl, whisk together the eggs, non-dairy milk, oil, almond butter, liquid stevia and vanilla extract.

Pour the wet ingredients into the dry ingredients and mix until fully combined. Fold in the blueberries.

For each waffle, generously spray the heated waffle iron surface with coconut oil spray. Pour about 1/2 cup of batter into the center. Cook until the waffle iron says it's done, and then wait another minute or two, (if you like a crispier waffle). Continue until all the batter is done. Serve warm.

I like serving with Berry Syrup.

Berry Pancakes

These pancakes are a regular in my household. I make a batch for my family and my personal chef clients every single week.

Makes 2 – 4 servings

Ingredients:

1 cup brown rice flour
1/2 cup arrowroot or tapioca starch/flour
2 Tablespoons xylitol
1 and 1/2 teaspoons baking powder
1/2 teaspoon baking soda
1/2 teaspoon sea salt
1/2 teaspoon xanthan gum
2 eggs
1 (13.5-ounce) can full fat coconut cream, or about 1 and 3/4 cups unsweetened non-dairy milk*
3 Tablespoons olive, coconut or avocado oil
1 teaspoon vanilla extract, (optional)*
6 drops liquid stevia
1 cup fresh berries of your choice, chopped to small bite-sized pieces.
Coconut oil spray or grass-fed butter

Directions:

In a large bowl, mix together the brown rice flour, tapioca starch, xylitol, baking powder, baking soda, sea salt, and xanthan gum. Use a whisk to get rid of any lumps. In a blender, combine the eggs, coconut cream, oil, vanilla extract, if using, and liquid stevia. Pour the wet ingredients into the dry ingredients and whisk until well combined. Gently fold in the chopped berries.

Heat a skillet over medium heat. Once heated, either spray with coconut oil spray or grease with grass-fed butter and turn heat down to low. Pour about 1/4 cup batter at a time onto the skillet and cook each side for a few minutes until golden brown.**

Continue until all the batter is done. Serve warm.

I like serving with Berry Syrup.

****If batter is too thick, add filtered water, 1 Tablespoon at a time, until a looser batter is formed. Option to use unsweetened non-dairy milk.***
*****Pancakes should be cooked slowly at a low temperature to avoid burning. If this process takes too long on one pan, either use a large griddle to cook multiple pancakes at once or heat two pans and cook pancakes simultaneously.***

Berry Pancakes

*

Berry "Syrup"

Waffles and pancakes can be enjoyed as-is but this berry "syrup" recipe is here for when you want to go the extra mile.

Makes about 1/2 cup

Ingredients:
1/3 cup berries of your choice
2 Tablespoons unsweetened almond or coconut milk
1 teaspoon xylitol
2 drops liquid stevia
1/2 teaspoon vanilla (optional)
1 small dash xanthan gum (optional)*
Pinch sea salt

Directions:
Place all of the ingredients into a blender and starting on low speed, start to blend, slowly increasing speed until everything is fully blended. Store in an airtight container with a fitted lid in the fridge for 5 – 7 days.

Xanthan gum added to this will help keep the syrup loose and easy to pour.

Almond Butter Drizzle

This almond butter drizzle will add a touch of sweetness and a boost of protein.

Makes about 1/2 cup

Ingredients:
1/4 cup unsweetened almond or coconut milk*
2 Tablespoons almond butter**
1/2 teaspoon xylitol
1/2 teaspoon vanilla (optional)
Pinch sea salt

Directions:
Place everything into a small bowl and whisk to combine. If you would like it thicker, add more almond butter. If you prefer it thinner, add more almond or coconut milk.

Store in an airtight container with a fitted lid in the fridge for 5 – 7 days.

Add more non-dairy milk for a thinner drizzle.
*****Option to use your favorite nut or seed butter in place of almond butter.***

Strawberry and Cream Parfait

Whipping fresh strawberries together with full fat coconut cream creates a light and fluffy strawberry whipped cream. Even my 1-year old daughter enjoys it!

Makes about 2 cups

Ingredients:
2 cups fresh strawberries
1 (13.5-ounce) can full-fat coconut cream*
1/4 cup chia seeds
6 drops liquid stevia
Pinch sea salt

Parfait additions:
Fresh berries
Nuts of choice
Unsweetened shredded coconut

Directions:
Place the strawberries in a food processor and give them a quick pulse. Now scrape down the sides of the food processor, add the coconut cream, chia seeds, liquid stevia, and sea salt and process until fully combined.

Taste for seasoning and add more stevia if desired.

Pour into a container with a fitted lid and place in the fridge to set for about 2 – 3 hours, or overnight. This should firm up and get slightly thick.

Eat as is or create a parfait by layering the coconut cream, fresh berries, nuts of choice and shredded coconut into a small serving bowl, jar, or glass. Continue layering several times and enjoy.

Do NOT use the Trader Joe's brand of coconut cream. Their coconut cream is too watery and clumpy for this recipe.

Nutty Power Granola

This granola packs a real punch. It's high in protein, grain free and perfect for those mornings when you need your breakfast to have a little more sticking power.

Makes 3 - 4 cups

Ingredients:
1 cup raw almonds, chopped
1 cup raw pecans, chopped
1 cup raw walnuts, chopped
1 cup unsweetened shredded coconut
1 teaspoon ground cinnamon
1/2 teaspoon sea salt
3 Tablespoons coconut oil
3 Tablespoons xylitol
1 teaspoon vanilla extract
20 drops liquid stevia

Additional Ingredients when Served:
Non-diary milk
Fresh berries of choice

Directions:

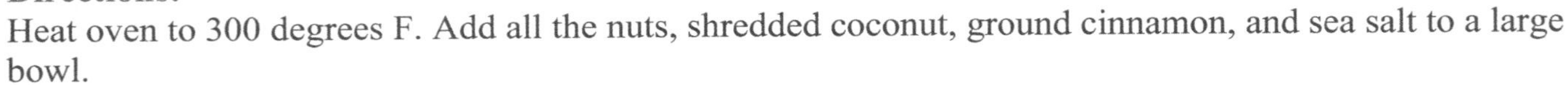

Heat oven to 300 degrees F. Add all the nuts, shredded coconut, ground cinnamon, and sea salt to a large bowl.

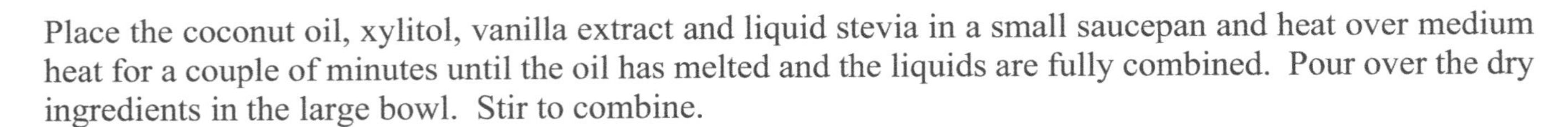

Place the coconut oil, xylitol, vanilla extract and liquid stevia in a small saucepan and heat over medium heat for a couple of minutes until the oil has melted and the liquids are fully combined. Pour over the dry ingredients in the large bowl. Stir to combine.

Line a baking sheet with parchment paper and evenly spread the granola on it. Bake for 8 - 10 minutes, then stir granola on sheet and bake for another 10 minutes or until golden brown.

Serve 1 cup of granola with unsweetened almond or coconut milk and fresh berries of choice.

Store leftover granola in an airtight container with a fitted lid in the fridge for 3 - 4 weeks or in the freezer for up to 3 months.

Vanilla Granola

Here's your new favorite not-too-sweet granola recipe that's quick and easy to make. Having pre-made granola on hand in your fridge or freezer can be a life saver on those mornings or afternoons when you need a quick bite but don't have the time to prepare anything.

Makes 5 cups

Ingredients:
3 cups gluten-free rolled oats
1 and 1/2 cups raw almonds, chopped
1 cup unsweetened shredded coconut
2 Tablespoons xylitol
1/2 teaspoon sea salt
1/4 cup plus 2 Tablespoons coconut oil (6 Tablespoons total)
2 teaspoons vanilla extract
6 drops liquid stevia
Unsweetened coconut or almond milk for serving

Directions:
Heat oven to 325 degrees F. and line a baking sheet with parchment paper. Set aside. Add the oats, chopped almonds, shredded coconut, xylitol, and sea salt to a large mixing bowl. Stir to combine.

Place the coconut oil, vanilla and liquid stevia in a small saucepan and heat over medium heat for a couple of minutes until the oil has melted and the liquids are fully combined. Pour over the dry ingredients and combine everything together.

Spread the granola evenly over your prepared baking sheet. Bake for 6 minutes, then stir granola on the baking sheet and bake for another 6 minutes, or until golden brown. Enjoy with unsweetened coconut or almond milk.

Store leftover granola in an airtight container with a fitted lid in the fridge for 3 - 4 weeks or in the freezer for up to 3 months.

Garlic, Spinach and Sweet Potato Quiche

Don't let the word Quiche intimidate you. This recipe is doable for even the novice chef. I like to serve this as a breakfast on its own, or as an entrée alongside a big leafy green salad.

Makes 6 servings

Ingredients:

Crust:

Olive or coconut oil spray for greasing pie dish
1 and 1/2 cups almond meal
1/2 cup brown rice or sweet sorghum flour
1/2 teaspoon sea salt
1/3 cup olive oil
1 egg

Filling:

7 eggs
2 Tablespoons filtered water
2 Tablespoons olive oil
4 garlic cloves, minced
1/3 cup sweet potato, small cube
1/2 teaspoon sea salt, divided
1/2 cup spinach

Directions:

Preheat oven to 400°F. and grease a pie dish generously with oil and set aside.

For the crust, whisk together the almond meal, brown rice or sorghum flour, and sea salt in a medium size bowl. In a separate, smaller bowl, whisk together the oil and egg and pour into the bowl of dry ingredients. Stir to combine. Pat this batter into the greased pie dish, using your hands to spread it evenly around the bottom and up the sides. The crust should be about 1/8 – 1/4 inch thick. Poke the entire crust with a fork to prevent bubbles when baking. Bake for 15 minutes. Remove from heat and set aside.

In the meantime, make the filling by whisking together the eggs and water in a large bowl and set aside.

Heat a skillet over medium heat and add 2 Tablespoons olive oil. Add the garlic, sweet potato and a pinch of sea salt. Sauté for 3 - 5 minutes, stirring constantly to keep the garlic from burning. Add the spinach and remaining sea salt and sauté for 1 minute more.

Gently stir the potato mixture into the egg mixture and pour into the prepared crust. Bake for about 30 minutes or until the center is firm to the touch. Remove from oven and let cool for about 10 minutes before cutting.

Leek and Onion Quiche

I enjoy quiche so much that I decided to include another variation. Leeks and onions are my favorite combination to add to eggs in the morning. Giving them a quick sauté takes away the spicy bite and leaves them nice and sweet.

Makes 6 servings

Ingredients:

Crust:

Olive or coconut oil spray for greasing pie dish
1 and 1/2 cups almond meal
1/2 cup brown rice or sweet sorghum flour
1/2 teaspoon sea salt
2 Tablespoons fresh or dried rosemary, minced
1/3 olive oil
1 egg

Filling:

7 eggs
2 Tablespoons filtered water
2 Tablespoons olive oil
1 cup yellow onion, small dice
1/2 teaspoon sea salt, divided
2 cups leek, cut in thin half moons

Directions:

Preheat oven to 400°F. Grease a pie dish generously with oil and set aside.

For the crust, whisk together the almond meal, brown rice or sorghum flour, sea salt, and rosemary in a medium size bowl. In a separate, smaller bowl, whisk together the oil and egg and pour into the bowl of dry ingredients. Stir to combine. Pat this batter into the greased pie dish, using your hands to spread it evenly around the bottom and up the sides. The crust should be about 1/8 – 1/4 inch thick. Poke the entire crust with a fork to prevent bubbles when baking. Bake for 15 minutes. Remove from heat and set aside.

In the meantime, make the filling by whisking together the eggs and water in a large bowl and set aside. Heat a large skillet over medium heat with 2 Tablespoons of olive oil and add the onion and 1/8 teaspoon of sea salt. Sauté for 2 – 3 minutes, or until the onions start to soften. Add the leeks and remaining sea salt and sauté for a couple minutes more.

Gently stir the leek mixture into the egg mixture and pour into the prepared crust. Bake for about 30 minutes or until the center is firm to the touch. Remove from oven and let cool for about 10 minutes before cutting.

Enjoy warm.

Spinach and Onion Frittata

(Made in a cast iron skillet)

Frittatas are a fun way to use up any leftover veggies that are sitting in your fridge. They're also quick to make and taste delicious.

Makes 4 – 6 servings

Ingredients:
6 – 7 eggs
2 Tablespoons filtered water
Olive oil or grass-fed butter for sautéing
1/2 medium size red onion, diced
3 cloves fresh garlic, minced
1/2 teaspoon sea salt
1 cup fresh spinach
2 green onions (white and green parts), finely minced
Pinch black pepper

Directions:
Preheat oven to broil setting. Whisk eggs and filtered water and set aside.

Heat a well-seasoned 12-inch cast iron sauté pan with butter or olive oil over medium heat. Add red onion, garlic, and sea salt and sauté for a couple of minutes, making sure the garlic does not burn. Next add the fresh spinach and give a quick stir. Pour egg mixture into the pan and stir one more time. Sprinkle with fresh green onions and a pinch of black pepper.

Cook for about 4 – 5 minutes, or until the egg mixture starts to set on the bottom. Using an oven glove, remove the skillet from the burner and place in the broiler for about 4 – 5 minutes more, or until lightly browned and fluffy. Let this cool for a couple minutes before slicing.

Enjoy warm.

*

Spinach and Onion Frittata

(Made in a pie dish)

No everyone has a cast iron skillet, so I have included directions on how to make a frittata in a pie dish.

Makes 4 – 6 servings

Ingredients:
1 Tablespoon olive oil or grass-fed butter, more to grease pie dish
6 – 7 eggs
2 Tablespoons filtered water
1/2 medium size red onion, diced
3 cloves fresh garlic, peeled and minced
1/2 teaspoon sea salt
1 cup fresh spinach
2 green onions (white and green parts), finely minced
Pinch black pepper

Directions:
Preheat oven to 350 degrees F. and generously oil a standard 9-inch pie dish.

Whisk eggs and filtered water in a large mixing bowl and set aside.

Heat a large skillet over medium heat with 1 Tablespoon butter or olive oil. Add red onion, garlic, and sea salt and sauté for a couple of minutes, making sure the garlic does not burn. Next add the fresh spinach and give a quick stir. Remove skillet from heat and add sautéed veggies to the egg mixture in the large mixing bowl. Give a quick stir. Pour all of this into the greased pie dish and sprinkle with fresh green onions and a pinch of black pepper.

Cook for about 20 - 25 minutes, or until firm to the touch in the center. Remove from the oven and let cool for a couple minutes before slicing.

Enjoy warm.

Scrambled Eggs with Basil and Avocado

I enjoyed this recipe for breakfast almost every morning the first few weeks after my daughter was born. The combination of protein and fat from the eggs and avocado helped me feel full and satisfied for hours on end.

Makes 2 servings

Ingredients:
6 large organic, free-range eggs
2 Tablespoons filtered water
2 pinches sea salt, divided
1 Tablespoon olive or coconut oil
1/4 cup red onion, small dice
1 avocado, diced
1/4 cup packed fresh basil, minced
Pinch black pepper

Directions:
In a medium size bowl, whisk the eggs and filtered until combined.

Heat a medium non-stick skillet with 1 Tablespoon of oil over medium-low heat. When the pan is hot, add diced onions and a pinch of sea salt. Sauté for a couple minutes until the onions start to turn translucent. Now add the whisked egg mixture and another pinch of sea salt. As the eggs begin to set, gently pull the eggs across the pan with a wooden spoon, forming large soft curds.

Continue cooking and pulling the eggs and folding them into each other until the eggs have cooked and there is no more liquid. Do this gently and do NOT stir constantly. Turn off the heat and gently fold in the avocado, basil, and a pinch of black pepper.

Enjoy warm.

Eggs Over Easy with Shredded Brussels Sprouts

I love shredding brussels sprouts because they become more flavorful and less likely to make you gassy. Pairing them with good quality, pasture raised eggs makes this dish a high protein, grain free breakfast that can also be served for lunch or dinner.

Makes 2 servings

Ingredients:
12 medium size Brussels Sprouts
1/4 cup of olive oil, coconut oil or unsalted grass-fed butter, divided
1/2 yellow onion, sliced into half moons
1/2 teaspoon sea salt, divided
2 teaspoons caraway seeds (optional)
2 Tablespoons apple cider vinegar
Filtered water
2 Tablespoons sunflower seeds (roasted and salted)
4 eggs
Pinch black pepper

Directions:
Trim ends off Brussels sprouts and cut into thin slices from the top part of the sprout, slicing down toward the trimmed end. Set aside.

Heat a large skillet with 2 Tablespoons oil or butter and place the sliced onions in the pan with a pinch of sea salt and caraway seeds (if using). Sauté on medium heat for 3 - 4 minutes, or until the onions start to soften. Next add the shredded Brussels Sprouts with another pinch of sea salt and sauté for a couple more minutes stirring around to coat everything with the oil or butter. Add the apple cider vinegar, give it a quick stir, and place a fitted lid over the top to create steam. Continue to sauté, stirring occasionally until the Brussels Sprouts are soft, about 5 - 10 minutes. If the Brussels Sprouts start to stick, add filtered water 1 Tablespoon at a time to unstick and continue creating steam. Finally, stir in sunflower seeds and turn off heat.

Heat a separate, medium size non-stick skillet over medium-low heat and add 2 Tablespoons of oil or butter. Once the oil is hot, crack the eggs into the pan*. Sprinkle eggs with a pinch of sea salt and pepper. Once the whites start to set and go from translucent to white, gently lift one side and flip the egg over, avoiding breaking the yolk. Cook for about 1 minute more. Slide onto plates and serve warm with Brussels sprout and onion mix.

If you have a smaller pan, you may want to cook the eggs 2 at a time.

Eggs Over Easy with Sautéed Kale

During my studies in culinary school I made leafy greens a staple for breakfast. I've managed to keep that up all these years later since it keeps me feeling light and flexible. If you've never eaten veggies for breakfast, I encourage you to give it a try.

Makes 1 serving

Ingredients:
2 Tablespoons grass-fed butter, divided
2 room temperature eggs
1/4 teaspoon sea salt, divided
Pinch black pepper
2 cups kale, chopped
1 Tablespoon apple cider vinegar
1/2 avocado, sliced

Directions:
Heat 1 Tablespoon of butter in a non-stick skillet over medium heat. Once butter is warm, crack eggs into skillet. Sprinkle with a generous pinch of sea salt. Once the egg white is no longer opaque, use a spatula to gently flip the eggs, being careful not to break the yolk. Cook for about 1 minute more. Carefully remove the eggs from the skillet and sprinkle with black pepper.

In the same skillet, add 1 more Tablespoon of butter and over medium heat add the kale, apple cider vinegar and another 1/8 teaspoon of sea salt and sauté the kale for about 2 to 3 minutes, or until it has softened.

Pour this onto a plate and top with eggs and sliced avocado. Enjoy warm.

Main Dishes

"Start where you are. Use what you have. Do what you can."

- Arthur Ashe

Salmon Salad

A personal chef client of mine had this dish at a restaurant and liked it so much he begged me to recreate it. It's a unique way to serve salmon and can be enjoyed on a bed of lettuce, with sliced veggies or in cassava tortillas as shown below.

Makes 2 – 3 servings

Ingredients:
1-pound fresh salmon
1 Tablespoon olive oil
Zest of one lemon
1/4 teaspoon sea salt, plus 1 pinch
1/3 cup Persian cucumber*, small dice
1/4 - 1/3 cup red onion, small dice
1/4 cup celery, small dice
1 teaspoon fresh or dried dill, minced
1/4 cup ***Homemade Mayonnaise (see recipe)***, more if desired
Juice of one lemon
Pinch black pepper

Directions:
Preheat oven to 350 degrees F. and line a baking sheet with parchment paper.

Place fish skin side down on lined baking sheet and drizzle with olive oil, lemon zest and a pinch of sea salt. Bake for about 10 – 12 minutes or until easily flaked with a fork in the center.**

Place the cucumber, red onion, celery and dill in a large mixing bowl. Once the salmon is finished cooking, let cool for about 5 minutes, peel away the skin, and crumble the fish into the same mixing bowl, being careful to remove any bones. Add the homemade mayonnaise, lemon juice, 1/4 teaspoon of sea salt and pinch of black pepper. Use a fork to finish crumbling the fish and combine all of the ingredients together.

Serve over leafy greens or wrapped in ***Cassava Tortillas.***

****I prefer Persian cucumbers because they are less watery.***
*****Cooking time will vary depending on the size of your fish.***

Matt's Favorite Shepherd's Pie

Matt is my husband, and I think the name of this dish says it all! ☺

Makes 4 servings

Ingredients:

Filling:

1 Tablespoon olive oil
1 cup red onion, small dice
6 – 8 cloves garlic, minced
1/4 teaspoon sea salt, divided
1 cup frozen spinach
1 cup broccoli, small chop
1/2-pound ground beef, bison, or turkey
1 (14.5-ounce) can diced tomatoes
2 teaspoons tapioca flour

Topping:

2 cups white sweet potato*, washed and cubed
3 cups cauliflower, chopped
6 cloves garlic
1 (13.5-ounce) can coconut milk
1/4 teaspoon sea salt, more if desired
Filtered water
4 Tablespoons grass-fed butter
Pinch black pepper
2 green onions, minced

Directions:

For the filling, in a large skillet, heat the olive oil over medium heat. Add the red onion, garlic, and a pinch of sea salt. Sauté for 2 – 3 minutes, stirring constantly. Next add the frozen spinach, chopped broccoli and another pinch of sea salt and sauté for 3 – 4 minutes more. Remove from heat and pour contents into a large mixing bowl, using a spatula.

In the same skillet, over medium heat, add the ground meat of choice and another pinch of sea salt. Start crumbling the meat using a wooden spoon. Continue to sauté and crumble until the meat is almost cooked through. Add the can of diced tomatoes and give it a quick stir with the meat. Add this to the mixing bowl with the onion mixture. Finally add the tapioca flour and mix to combine everything evenly. Pour into an 8 x 8-inch baking dish and set aside. Preheat oven to 350 degrees F. and place oven rack to the middle shelf.

For the topping, in a medium size saucepan add the sweet potato, cauliflower, garlic, coconut milk, and sea salt. Add filtered water to just cover the top of the veggies. Bring to a boil, cover with a fitted lid, and reduce heat to medium-low. Simmer for 10 – 15 minutes, or until the sweet potato is pierceable with a fork. Remove from heat.

If there is excess liquid, use a slotted spoon to remove the potatoes, cauliflower, and garlic cloves from the saucepan and place in a large mixing bowl. Add the butter and black pepper. Using a potato masher, mash until creamy and everything is fully incorporated. Mix in the green onions and taste for seasoning. Add more salt if necessary.

Spread the potato mixture on top of the ground meat and veggie mix in the baking dish. Bake for 50 – 60 minutes, or until golden brown and bubbling.

If sweet potato is organic, no need to peel.

Matt's Favorite Shepherd's Pie

Chicken Salad with Collard Green Wraps

Collard greens are not as bitter as kale, and when blanched they become soft and bendy. Blanched collard greens make the perfect vehicle for things like chicken or salmon salad.

Makes 2 – 3 servings

Ingredients:
1/2-pound cooked chicken breast
1/3 cup Persian cucumber*, small dice
1/4 - 1/3 cup red onion, small dice
1/4 cup celery, small dice
1/4 cup carrot, small dice
1 Tablespoon fresh parsley, minced
1 green onion, minced
3 – 4 Tablespoons ***Homemade Mayonnaise (see recipe)***
1/4 - 1/2 teaspoon sea salt
Pinch black pepper
4 large (or 6 small) collard green leaves
Sliced avocado

Directions:
Place the cooked chicken in a food processor and pulse several times to break up then add to a mixing bowl. Add the remaining ingredients using a fork to mix everything together. Taste for seasoning.

Wash collard green leaves and carefully remove the stems using a sharp knife. Discard stems or save for another time. Bring a medium size pot of water to a boil. Once the water is boiling, blanch the leaves by placing them in the hot water for about 5 seconds. Use a slotted spoon to carefully remove from the boiling water. Pat dry with a towel and set aside.

To serve, take a collard wrap, place a scoop of chicken salad in the middle, top with a slice of avocado and wrap like a burrito. Enjoy.

I prefer Persian cucumbers because they are less watery.
*****Cooking time will vary depending on the size of your chicken breast.***

Egg Salad with Lettuce Wraps

I've heard romaine lettuce referred to as "a waste of time" because it's thought to have no nutrients. That's nonsense. From an energetic perspective, romaine lettuce helps keep you light and airy. It's extremely hydrating and low in calories making it perfect on hot summer days.

Makes 2 servings

Ingredients:

For the salad:

4 hard-boiled eggs, peeled
1/4 cup ***Homemade Mayonnaise (see recipe)***
1/4 cup red onion, finely chopped
2 Tablespoons celery, finely chopped
1 teaspoon dill, freshly minced
1/2 teaspoon sea salt
1/4 teaspoon smoked paprika
Generous pinch black pepper

Wraps:

8 – 10 lettuce leaves, washed and dried

Directions:

Place all of the egg salad ingredients into a mixing bowl and use a fork to break apart the eggs and mix everything together. Taste for seasoning.

To serve, take a lettuce leaf, place a scoop of egg salad in the middle. Wrap like a burrito and enjoy.

Marinated Kale Salad

Raw kale can be difficult for people to digest, especially those struggling with Candida. Massaging kale is an easy way to make it more digestible and flavorful. This is another go-to recipe in my house.

Makes 2 servings

*

Ingredients:

For the salad:

1 large bunch of Lacinato kale (about 4 cups)
Zest of 1 lemon
1/3 cup sun-dried tomatoes, in oil

Dressing:

2 Tablespoons olive oil
1 Tablespoon apple cider vinegar
1/4 teaspoon sea salt
Juice of 1 lemon

Fold-Ins:

1/4 cup pumpkin or sunflower seeds
1/2 avocado, diced

Directions:

Wash and dry kale leaves. Remove the stems by holding the end of the stem with one hand and pulling the leaf off towards the top end with the other hand. Set the stems aside for use at another time. Chop kale leaves into bite-size pieces and place in large bowl. Zest lemon over leaves and pour in the sun-dried tomatoes (allowing a little oil from the sun-dried tomato jar to go in as well).

In a separate smaller bowl, make the dressing my whisking together the olive oil, lemon juice, apple cider vinegar, and sea salt. Pour mixture over kale.* Using your hands, massage the mixture into the leaves for about 2 - 3 minutes. You will see and feel the kale getting softer in your hands. Finally, add the pumpkin or sunflower seeds and diced avocado on top. Taste for seasoning.

If you are wary of overdressing, try pouring half of the mixture in at first, then adding more as needed. There should be enough liquid to dress all the kale leaves, but not so much that it pools in the bottom of the bowl.

***I like serving with* Baked Chicken *or* Baked Salmon.**

Quinoa Tabbouleh

Tabbouleh is one of my favorite ways to prepare Quinoa. Traditionally made with wheat, this version is equally delicious and gluten free.

Makes 4 Servings

Ingredients:
1 cup tri-colored quinoa*
1 cup water or vegetable broth (no sugar added)
1/2 teaspoon sea salt, plus a pinch
2 Tablespoons olive oil
1 Tablespoon fresh lemon juice
1 Tablespoon apple cider vinegar
Pinch black pepper
2 green onions (green and white parts), finely diced
1/4 cup Persian cucumbers**, very small dice
1 handful parsley, minced (about 2 Tablespoons)
1 handful cilantro, minced (about 2 Tablespoons)
1 handful mint, minced (optional)
1/4 cup roasted and salted sunflower seeds

Directions:
Place the quinoa in a fine mesh strainer and rinse thoroughly under cool water to remove any dirt and loosen bitter coating. Place quinoa in a small saucepan with 1 cup water or broth and a pinch of sea salt. Bring the liquid to a boil, then cover and reduce heat to low and let simmer for 15 minutes. Turn off heat but keep the lid on the quinoa for another 5 minutes to prevent sticking to the bottom of the pan.

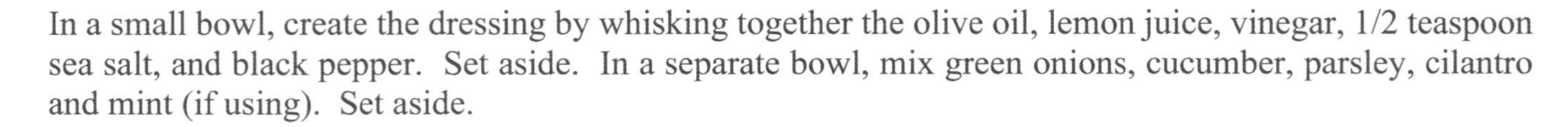

In a small bowl, create the dressing by whisking together the olive oil, lemon juice, vinegar, 1/2 teaspoon sea salt, and black pepper. Set aside. In a separate bowl, mix green onions, cucumber, parsley, cilantro and mint (if using). Set aside.

Place quinoa in a large mixing bowl and fluff with a fork (this keeps the dish light and airy). Slowly drizzle the dressing over the quinoa and fold in herbs and chopped vegetables. Add the sunflower seeds. Taste for seasoning.

***Any color quinoa will work; tri-color quinoa makes the dish extra enticing and colorful.**
****Persian cucumbers have less seeds and are less watery, making them great for a dish that calls for finely diced cucumbers.***

I like serving with Baked Salmon and Baked Veggies.

Seeded Veggie Burgers

What I love most about these veggie burgers is how easily they're made. Just throw everything into your food processor!

Makes 8 - 10 patties, depending on size

Ingredients:

Veggie Burgers:

Olive or coconut oil spray
1 cup raw sunflower seeds (soaking optional*)
1 cup raw pumpkin seeds (soaking optional*)
1/3 cup sun-dried tomatoes in oil
1/2 cup grated carrot
3 Tablespoons olive oil
1 teaspoon garlic powder
1/2 teaspoon sea salt
2 Tablespoons fresh parsley, minced
2 Tablespoons green onions, minced

For serving:

8 - 10 large lettuce leaves
1 avocado, sliced
1 beef tomato, sliced
Red onion slices

Directions:

Preheat oven to 350 degrees F. and line a baking sheet with parchment paper and lightly grease with olive or coconut oil spray. Place the sunflower and pumpkin seeds in a fine mesh strainer and rinse under cool water to remove any dust or debris, then place them in a food processor. Add the sun-dried tomatoes, allowing some of the oil to drip in, grated carrot, olive oil, garlic powder, and sea salt. Pulse until it forms a thick batter. This may take several minutes, and you may need to occasionally pause to scrape down the sides of the food processor.

Add the parsley and green onions and pulse again until fully combined. Taste for seasoning. Form the batter into patties and place onto your prepared baking sheet. Bake for about 10 - 15 minutes, or until golden brown. Remove from tray and let cool on a cooling rack. Serve on a large lettuce leaf with additional toppings such as slices of avocado, tomato, and red onion.

If soaking, place sunflower and pumpkin seeds in a medium sized bowl and cover with filtered water. Cover with a piece of cheese cloth or paper towel and allow to soak on your counter for 4 – 8 hours. Drain and rinse under faucet water in a fine mesh colander and proceed with the recipe.

I like serving with Baked Sweet Potato Fries and Homemade Ketchup.

Herbed Meatballs

The herbs in these meatballs keep them light and flavorful while the tomato paste keeps them moist. Turkey meatballs are one of my daughters' favorite foods.

Makes about 15 - 20 meatballs, depending on size

Ingredients:

1 Tablespoon olive oil for baking sheet
1-pound ground turkey, beef, bison or lamb
1/4 cup red onion, minced
2 Tablespoons fresh parsley or basil, minced
3 Tablespoons coconut flour
2 Tablespoons tomato paste*
1 egg, room temperature
1 teaspoon garlic powder
1/2 teaspoon sea salt
1/4 teaspoon black pepper

Directions:

Preheat oven to 350 degrees F. and line a baking sheet with foil or parchment paper and grease with 1 Tablespoon olive oil.

Place the ground meat in a large mixing bowl. Add the red onion, parsley or basil, coconut flour, tomato paste, egg, garlic powder, sea salt and black pepper. Mix thoroughly (I like using gloved hands), until everything is evenly incorporated.

Roll into balls about 1 rounded Tablespoon in size. Place on the oiled baking sheet and bake for 15 - 18 minutes, or until the center is no longer pink.

Option to use pumpkin puree.

***I like serving with* Sautéed Collard Greens.**

Mountain High Salad

This salad is incredibly healthy, beautiful and delicious. If you don't have a spirilzer, you can shred fresh beets, but beet "noodles" look oh so pretty.

Makes 2 servings

Ingredients:

Quinoa:

1 cup quinoa*
1 cup filtered water
2 pinches sea salt, divided
1 Tablespoon olive oil
2 teaspoons apple cider vinegar
1 Tablespoon lemon juice
Pinch black pepper

Salad:

4 cups leafy greens
1/3 cup cherry tomatoes
1 small carrot
1 small red beet
1/4 cup almonds, chopped

Dressing:

1/4 cup olive oil
2 Tablespoons filtered water
1 Tablespoon raw coconut aminos
Juice of 1 lime
1 (1-inch) piece fresh ginger, peeled and chopped
4 sprigs fresh mint or cilantro
1/4 teaspoon sea salt
2 drops liquid stevia (optional)

Directions:

Rinse the quinoa and place into a small saucepan with 1 cup filtered water and a pinch of sea salt. Bring to a boil, cover with a fitted lid and reduce the heat to low, cook for 15 minutes. Turn off the heat and let sit for 5 minutes before removing the lid to prevent sticking. Add the olive oil, apple cider vinegar, lemon juice, another pinch of sea salt, and black pepper to the quinoa and fluff with a fork.

Place the quinoa on the bottom of 2 serving bowls. Top each serving bowl with about 2 cups of leafy greens. Wash cherry tomatoes and cut in half and split between each salad. Wash and shred 1 carrot and split between each salad. Take the beet and cut off the top. Wash and spiralize. If you do not have a spiralizer, shred the same way you did the carrot. Divide the beet between each salad as well. Finish by sprinkling chopped almonds onto each salad.

To prepare the dressing, place all the ingredients into a high-powered blender. Blend, starting on low and work up to high speed, until creamy. Drizzle over each salad.

I love tri-colored quinoa for this recipe because of the variety in colors, but any color quinoa works!

Mountain High Salad

*

Italian Spaghetti Squash

Spaghetti squash is a fun way to replace noodles in your diet. I once served this to my husband's grandmother who asked if it was angel hair pasta. Too funny!

Makes 2 – 4 servings

Ingredients:
1 spaghetti squash
2 Tablespoons olive oil, divided
1/4 teaspoon sea salt
1 medium size red onion, cut into half moons
4 – 5 cloves garlic, minced
2 - 3 Tablespoons sunflower seeds
2 Tablespoons fresh basil, minced
Pinch black pepper

Directions:
Preheat oven to 350 degrees F and line a baking sheet with foil.

Cut spaghetti squash in half, longways, remove seeds and rub 1/2 Tablespoon olive oil on the inside of each half, sprinkle each side with a pinch of sea salt. Place cut side down on baking sheet and bake for about 30 – 45 minutes, or until the inside is soft and easily pierceable with a fork. Remove from oven and let cool slightly so you can handle it.

In the meantime, heat a medium size skillet over medium heat with 1 Tablespoon olive oil. Add onions, garlic and a pinch of sea salt. Sauté for about 2 – 3 minutes or until the onions soften. Add to a large mixing bowl.

Once the squash is cool enough to handle, take a fork and scrape out the strands which will become your "spaghetti" and place this in the same bowl with the onions and garlic. Add sunflower seeds, fresh basil, another pinch of sea salt, and black pepper. Stir to combine.

Taste for seasoning.

If you're having a hard time cutting the spaghetti squash in half, try using a fork to poke it with holes all over and then place it in the microwave for 3 – 5 minutes.

I like serving with Herbed Meatballs or Baked Salmon.

Slightly "Caesar" Salad

Although totally optional, I absolutely love the addition of Nori Seaweed in this recipe. Nori adds a salty flavor and a nutritional punch. It contains minerals and trace minerals, vitamin B12 and iodine.

Makes 2 large salads

Ingredients:

Salad Dressing:

1/4 cup filtered water
1/4 cup olive oil
2 Tablespoons fresh lemon juice
2 Tablespoons unsalted all-natural almond or tahini butter
1 Tablespoon raw coconut aminos
3 cloves garlic
1/4 teaspoon sea salt

Salad:

2 cups leafy greens
1/2 cup Persian cucumbers, diced
1/4 cup shredded carrots
1/2 cup avocado, chopped
1 nori sheet, shredded (optional)

Directions:

Start by preparing the dressing. Put all the ingredients, starting with the liquids, into a blender. Starting on low speed, start to blend, slowly working up to high speed. Blend until smooth and creamy.
Store in an airtight glass container in the refrigerator for about 7 – 10 days.*

To assemble the salad for a single serving, lay a bed of 1 cup leafy greens, top with 1/4 cup diced cucumber, 2 Tablespoons shredded carrot, 1/4 cup chopped avocado and shredded nori (if using). Top with 2 Tablespoons of salad dressing.**

Save extra dressing in an airtight container in the freezer for up to 2 months.
*****If dressing is too thick, dilute with a little filtered water.***

I like serving with ***Baked Chicken*** *or* ***Baked Salmon.***

*

Indian Style Vegetable Korma

I totally get that an Indian dish may seem a bit intimidating. Even as a "trained" chef, I still get a little intimated by Indian cuisine, but I've become a pro at simplifying things and this dish is no different. I've recreated this Indian dish in a healthy way without sacrificing flavor.

Makes 4 Servings

Ingredients:
2 Tablespoons coconut oil
1/2 cup yellow onion, small dice
4 garlic cloves, minced
1 teaspoon fresh ginger, peeled and minced
1/2 teaspoon curry powder
1/2 teaspoon sea salt, divided
1 cup rutabaga or turnip, small cubes
1 cup sweet potatoes, small cubes
1/2 cup carrot, small dice
1/4 teaspoon black pepper
1 cup full-fat coconut cream
1/4 cup tomato paste (no sugar added)
1/4 cup almonds, chopped or slivered
4 sprigs fresh cilantro, chopped
2 Tablespoons green onions (white and green parts), minced

*

Directions:

Heat 2 Tablespoons coconut oil in a large skillet over medium heat. Add the onion, garlic, ginger, curry powder, and 1/4 teaspoon sea salt and sauté for a couple of minutes or until the vegetables become fragrant. Add the rutabaga, sweet potatoes, carrot, black pepper, and another 1/4 teaspoon of sea salt and sauté for about 5 minutes more. Stir constantly.

Now add the coconut cream and tomato paste and stir to fully combine. Cover with a tight-fitting lid and reduce heat to low. Simmer for about 10 minutes or until the sweet potatoes are tender. Remove from heat and fold in the almonds, cilantro and green onions just before serving. Serve over brown rice.

I like serving over Brown Rice with Baked Chicken.

Seasoned Butternut Squash Salad

The ingredient combination of this dish might surprise you, but rest assured this dish is a total winner! Chocked full of nutrients, this Roasted Butternut Squash Salad will be your new favorite dish!

Makes 4 servings

Ingredients:
1 medium to large butternut squash (about 4 cups when chopped)
1/4 cup olive oil, divided
3/4 teaspoon sea salt, divided
1/2 cup red onion, small dice
1/4 cup green onions (green and white parts), minced
1/4 cup almonds, chopped
1/4 cup pitted black olives (optional)
1/4 cup sun-dried tomatoes
2 Tablespoons fresh cilantro, minced
1 Tablespoon apple cider vinegar
Juice of 1 lemon
4 cups organic arugula (or your favorite leafy green)

*

Directions:
Preheat oven to 350 degrees F.

Peel and cube the butternut squash into bite size pieces and place in a large bowl. Try to make the pieces around the same size for even cooking. Add 2 Tablespoons of olive oil and 1/4 teaspoon sea salt and use your hands to combine with squash. Pour onto a baking sheet and spread the butternut squash around to avoid crowding the pieces together. Bake for 18 - 25 minutes, or until pierceable with a fork. Stir the squash on the baking sheet halfway through cooking.

Meanwhile, heat 1 Tablespoon of olive oil in a medium size skillet over medium heat. Add red onion and 1/4 teaspoon sea salt and sauté for a few minutes. As onion begins to turn translucent, add minced green onions and cook for 30 more seconds. Pour sautéed onions into large mixing bowl along with chopped almonds, black olives, sun-dried tomatoes, and cilantro. When the butternut squash has finished cooking, add to the large mixing bowl as well.

Finally, add the remaining 1 Tablespoon of oil, 1/4 teaspoon of sea salt, along with the vinegar, lemon juice, and black pepper to the mixing bowl and gently stir. Serve warm over a bed of arugula.

Garlic, Basil Sliders

A juicy burger recipe that's free of gluten, dairy, corn, soy and grain! These Garlic, Basil Sliders are easy to prepare and delicious!

Makes 4 - 6 Sliders

Ingredients:

Sliders:

1-pound ground turkey, beef, bison or lamb
1/4 cup fresh basil, minced
1/3 cup red onion, minced
3 - 4 garlic cloves, minced
1 Tablespoon tomato paste
1/2 teaspoon sea salt
1/2 teaspoon black pepper

Toppings:

6 - 8 large lettuce leaves
1 avocado, sliced
1 beefsteak tomato, sliced
Homemade ketchup (see recipe)

Directions:

Preheat oven to 350°F. Line a baking sheet with parchment paper.

Place the ground meat into a large mixing bowl and add the basil, red onion, garlic, sea salt, and black pepper.* Mix thoroughly with your hands to incorporate evenly. Make 4 – 6 round patties. Place patties on prepared baking sheet and bake for about 15 minutes or until the internal temperature reaches 165°F.

Place each patty in the center of a lettuce leaf and top with sliced tomato, sliced avocado, and homemade ketchup. Wrap and enjoy.

If using lean turkey, beef, bison, or lamb, add 1 Tablespoon olive oil.

I like serving with Baked Sweet Potato Fries.

Chili Con Carne

This chili recipe is perfect for cold winter days when you're craving warm, comforting food.

Makes about 4 large servings

Ingredients:
3 Tablespoons olive or coconut oil, divided
1 yellow onion, small dice
4 – 5 garlic cloves, minced
1/2 teaspoon sea salt, divided
2 celery ribs (sticks), diced
2 medium size carrots, diced
1 teaspoon cumin
1 teaspoon smoked paprika
1 (14.5-ounce) can diced tomatoes (no vinegar or sugar added)*
4 cups vegetable broth (no sugar added)**
1-pound ground turkey, beef, bison or lamb
Pinch black pepper
4 green onions (green and white parts), small dice, divided
1 avocado, sliced for garnish
1 dollop of ***Vegan "Sour Cream" (see recipe)***

Directions:
Heat a large soup pot with 2 Tablespoons oil over medium heat. Once hot, add the diced onion, garlic, and a pinch of sea salt and sauté for about 2 - 3 minutes. Next add the celery, carrots, cumin, smoked paprika, and another pinch of sea salt and sauté for about 3 - 4 minutes more. Add the diced tomatoes and vegetable broth and bring to a boil. Reduce heat to low, cover and cook until the vegetables are soft, about 10 - 15 minutes.

In the meantime, heat a large skillet with the remaining 1 Tablespoon of oil over medium heat and add the ground turkey with a pinch of sea salt and pepper. Sauté turkey, slowly breaking apart and crumbling with a wooden spoon. Continue to sauté until the turkey is almost fully cooked. This should take about 5 minutes. When the turkey is almost fully cooked, add it to the soup pot and stir to combine.

Let the soup simmer for about 2 - 3 minutes more. This will allow the turkey to finish cooking and for all the flavors to combine. Remove from heat and stir in most of the diced green onions.

To serve, place a large ladle of chili in a soup bowl with a dollop of ***Vegan "Sour Cream"*** and garnish with sliced avocado and the remaining green onions.

****Try Trader Joe's Organic Diced Tomatoes or several brands sold at Whole Foods, including Organic San Marzano Region Diced Tomatoes.***
*****Try Trader Joe's Organic Vegetable Broth, or Imagine Organic Vegetable Broth sold at Whole Foods***

Chili Con Carne

*

Shredded Kale and Quinoa Salad

This salad incorporates quinoa and kale to create a dairy-free, gluten-free and anti-candida twist on the traditional Caesar Salad. I like serving this as-is or with some grilled chicken.

Makes 2 – 4 servings

Ingredients:
1 cup filtered water
1 cup tri-colored quinoa, rinsed thoroughly
1/4 teaspoon sea salt, divided
2 Tablespoons olive oil, divided
1/2 medium size red onion, small dice
3 garlic cloves, minced
1/2 cup carrots, small dice
4 cups kale, cut into small pieces*
1 Tablespoon apple cider vinegar
1/4 cup sunflower seeds (I prefer roasted and salted)
2 Tablespoons minced fresh cilantro
Juice of one lemon

Directions:
Place water and quinoa in a small saucepan with a pinch of sea salt and bring to a boil. Cover with a fitted lid, reduce heat to low and simmer for 15 minutes. After 15 minutes, turn off the heat and let sit for another 5 minutes before removing the lid.

In the meantime, heat 1 Tablespoon of olive oil over medium heat in a large, non-stick skillet and sauté red onion and garlic with 1/8 teaspoon sea salt for 1 – 2 minutes, stirring constantly to prevent burning. Now add the carrots and sauté about 2 minutes more. Finally add the chopped kale, remaining 1/8 teaspoon sea salt, and apple cider vinegar. Cover with a fitted lid and let steam for about 2 minutes more.

Place all of the ingredients from the skillet into a large bowl and when quinoa is finished cooking, add that to the bowl as well as the sunflower seeds, cilantro, lemon juice and remaining olive oil. Using a fork, fluff the quinoa and stir everything to combine.**

I like to quickly pulse the kale in a food processor.
*****Option to toss this with* Caesar Salad Dressing.**

Stuffed Peppers

Stuffed peppers are a great way to wow dinner guests. The preparation is relatively simple, but they are beautiful when plated.

Makes 4 - 5 servings *

Ingredients:
Olive or coconut oil spray for baking sheet
4 bell peppers, cut in half and seeded
2 Tablespoons olive oil, divided
1/2-pound ground turkey, beef, bison, or lamb
1/2 teaspoon sea salt, divided
1/2 medium size yellow onion, chopped
3 garlic cloves, minced
1 (1-inch) piece fresh ginger, peeled and minced
1/2 cup zucchini, small dice
1 teaspoon dried basil and thyme
1 cup (packed) fresh spinach
1 (15-ounce) can diced tomatoes, drained

Directions:
Preheat oven to 350°F. Line a baking sheet with foil and spray with olive oil spray. Place the peppers face down and bake for 10 minutes. Remove from oven and set aside.

Heat a medium-sized nonstick skillet over medium heat with 1 Tablespoon of oil. After about 10 seconds, add your meat of choice and a pinch of sea salt. Break the meat into crumbles, stirring frequently, and cook until there is no pink meat remaining. Transfer to a large mixing bowl.

In the same skillet, heat 1 more Tablespoon of olive oil and add the onions, garlic, ginger, and a pinch of sea salt. Sauté mixture for 2 - 3 minutes, stirring frequently. Add the zucchini, basil and thyme, and another pinch of sea salt. Sauté a couple minutes more. Add the spinach, the can of diced tomatoes, and another pinch of sea salt. Sauté for about 2 – 3 minutes.

Add this mixture to the bowl of cooked meat and stir to combine. Spoon mixture into each pepper cavity, and place the peppers, stuffed side up, on the baking sheet. Bake for another 10 - 15 minutes or until the stuffing starts to turn golden brown.

I like serving with Brown Rice.

Zucchini Noodles

If you don't have a spiralizer you can always make your "noodles" using a vegetable peeler.

Makes 2 servings

Ingredients:
2 large zucchinis, washed
3 Tablespoons olive oil, divided
1/2 medium size red onion, cut into half moons
3 garlic cloves, minced
1/8 teaspoon sea salt, divided
1/3 cup sun-dried tomatoes, in olive oil
1 Tablespoon filtered water
3 Tablespoons fresh basil, minced
Juice of one lemon
Pinch black pepper

Directions:
If you have a spiralizer, use this to make your "noodles" from the zucchini. If you don't have a spiralizer, you can re-create similar noodles using a vegetable peeler to peel long strips of zucchini, starting from one end and peeling down to the other. Peel strips into a large bowl. Include the skin and peel all the way down until you reach the more fibrous and seedy middle of the zucchini, which you can discard.

Heat a large non-stick skillet over medium heat and add 2 Tablespoons of olive oil. Add the onions, garlic, and a pinch of sea salt and sauté for about 3 - 4 minutes. Next add the sun-dried tomatoes and sauté for 1 – 2 minutes more. Now add the zucchini noodles, another pinch of sea salt, the remaining olive oil, and filtered water. Stir well and then cover with a fitted lid to steam zucchini for about 4 - 5 minutes, or until noodles are soft. Add the basil, lemon juice, and black pepper. Stir to combine, then remove from heat. Serve warm.

I like serving with Baked Chicken or Herbed Meatballs.

Turkey and Cabbage Sauté

This Turkey and Cabbage Sauté is a dinnertime regular in my house. It's both light and filling at the same time. It gives a nod to Asian-inspired cuisine, and actually reminds me of those famous lettuce wraps at PF Chang's. Except without the gluten. And the soy. And the MSG.

Makes 2 – 4 servings

Ingredients:

2 Tablespoons olive oil, divided
1-pound ground turkey, dark or white meat
1/2 teaspoon sea salt, divided
1/2 cup medium size red onion, sliced into half moons
4 garlic cloves, minced
1 (1-inch) piece of fresh ginger, peeled and minced
2 cups shredded green or red cabbage
1 Tablespoon apple cider vinegar
1 Tablespoon coconut aminos
Juice of 1 lime
2 - 4 drops liquid stevia
2 green onions (white and green parts), minced
2 - 3 Tablespoons sunflower or sesame seeds
1 avocado, sliced for garnish

Directions:

Heat 1 teaspoon of oil over medium heat in a large nonstick skillet. Add the ground turkey and a pinch of sea salt and sauté, stirring constantly and crumbling the turkey, for about 5 – 10 minutes or until all of the meat is cooked and no longer pink. Remove turkey from the skillet and place into a large mixing bowl.

In the same skillet, add a Tablespoon of oil over medium heat and add the red onions, garlic, ginger and a pinch of sea and sauté for 2 – 3 minutes, stirring constantly, until the onions start to soften.

Add the shredded cabbage, apple cider vinegar, coconut aminos, lime juice, stevia and a pinch of sea salt and cover with a fitted lid. Let simmer for about 2 – 3 minutes. Remove the lid and using a wooden spatula sauté for a couple minutes more, or until the cabbage is soft and cooked.

Add this mixture to the ground turkey in the mixing bowl. Mix in the green onions and sunflower or sesame seeds and taste for seasoning. Garnish with sliced avocado.

Baked Salmon over Leafy Greens

Salmon is on the menu every week in my household. It's a nutritional powerhouse with impressive health benefits. This is a basic way to serve it, over leafy greens, but you could add some quinoa, brown rice or cassava tortillas to jazz it up.

Makes 2 – 3 servings

Ingredients:

Salmon:

Olive oil spray
1 pound fresh or frozen salmon, cut in half
2 Tablespoons grass-fed unsalted butter, cut in half
Zest of 1 lemon
1/8 teaspoon sea salt
Pinch black pepper
2 Tablespoons minced green onions, more for garnish

Dressing:

1 Tablespoon olive oil
2 teaspoons apple cider vinegar
Juice of one lemon
Pinch sea salt & black pepper

Salad:

2 cups spring green mix or arugula, washed
1 cucumber
1 tomato
1 avocado

Directions:

Preheat oven to 450 degrees F. Line a baking sheet with parchment paper and spray with olive oil spray. Set aside.

If salmon is frozen, place in cold water, while still in a sealed package, until it has thawed. This takes about 20 – 30 minutes. Place salmon skin side down on lined baking sheet and place each Tablespoon of butter on each salmon filet. Sprinkle the lemon zest, sea salt, pepper, and 1 Tablespoon of minced green onions evenly over both filets.

Bake until salmon is cooked through, about 10 – 15 minutes, depending on the cut of fish. In the meantime, place all of the salad dressing ingredients in a small bowl and whisk to combine. Set aside.

Place 1 cup of leafy greens on each plate, top with cucumber, tomatoes and avocado Once fish is done, place on top of the greens and garnish with another sprinkle of green onions and drizzle with dressing.

Butternut Squash and Black Bean Tacos

A totally plant-based taco recipe that's healthy, colorful and delicious. These tacos are great any day of the week.

Makes 2 servings

Ingredients:

Tacos:

2 Tablespoons olive or coconut oil
1/3 cup red onion, small dice
4 garlic cloves, minced
1 teaspoon cumin
1 teaspoon smoked paprika
1/2 teaspoon sea salt
2 cups butternut squash, small cubes
1 can black beans, rinsed
Juice of 1 lime (about 1 Tablespoon)
2 green onions (white and green parts), minced
4 sprigs cilantro, minced

Tortillas:
Makes 10 – 12 tortillas

1 cup cassava flour*
1/2 teaspoon sea salt
2/3 cup filtered water, room temperature**
2 Tablespoons olive oil

Toppings:

Sliced avocado

Directions:

Heat a large skillet over medium heat with 2 Tablespoons olive or coconut oil. Add the onions, garlic, cumin, smoked paprika and a pinch of sea salt. Sauté for 3 – 4 minutes, stirring constantly.

Add the butternut squash and another pinch of sea salt and continue to sauté for about 5 – 6 minutes more, or until butternut squash is easily pierceable with a fork (timing on this will vary depending on how big your cubes are). Add the black beans, lime juice and another pinch of sea salt. Give it a quick stir to combine fully and let simmer for about 2 – 3 minutes more. Remove from heat and add the green onions and cilantro.

To make the tortillas, combine all of the ingredients in a medium sized mixing bowl. The batter should not be too wet or too dry. If too wet, add more flour 1 teaspoon at a time. If too dry, add more water, 1 teaspoon at a time. Roll into balls about the size of a golf ball.

If using a tortilla press, line with parchment and press. If you do not have a tortilla press, you can use 2 pieces of parchment paper and place the batter in the middle and roll out using a rolling pin.

Heat a dry skillet over medium-high heat. Place tortilla on the hot skillet and allow to cook for about 30 seconds, flip over, and cook for 30 seconds more. Cool on a cooling rack. Continue until all the batter is gone.

I prefer Otto's brand of cassava flour.
****If the batter is too dry, add more filtered water 1 Tablespoon at a time until it is moist and holds together, yet doesn't stick to your hands.***

I like serving with Asian Coleslaw, Guacamole and Fresh Salsa.

Butternut Squash and Black Bean Tacos

DISCLAIMER

The recipes provided in this book have been created specifically for the ingredients and techniques called for. Natural Tasty Chef is not responsible for the user's specific health or allergy needs that may require supervision. The information, recipes, tips, and suggestions provided by Natural Tasty Chef in this book are not intended to be a substitute for the medical advice of a licensed physician.

*** *Select photos by Bobak Radbin: https://www.bobakradbin.com*

Printed in Great Britain
by Amazon